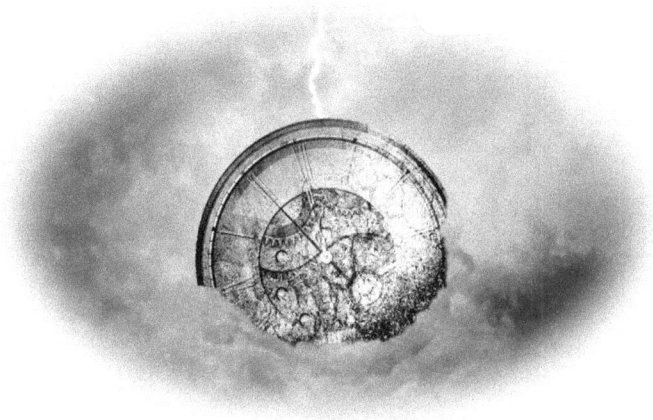

SURVIVING the WRITING APOCALYPSE

TANIA L. RAMOS

BLACKBIRD LSD

Cover design, interior book design
and eBook design
by Blue Harvest Creative
www.blueharvestcreative.com

Surviving the Writing Apocalypse

Published by
Blackbird LSD

ISBN-13: 978-0615791111
ISBN-10: 0615791115

Visit the author at:
Websites: *tanialramos.com* and *bestillnovel.com*
Blog: *newauthorpublishing.wordpress.com*
Facebook: *facebook.com/tanialramosbooks*
Twitter: *twitter.com/tanialramos*

Also by Tania L. Ramos
Be Still
When I Thought I Was Tough

Acknowledgements

I would like to thank my family who put up with my incessant psychosis while writing this manual. Many thanks go out to Patricia and Daniel at the Blackbird LSD offices for proofing and listening to me whine at all hours of the day and night. To all my friends who continue to support me and think I should write full-time, I say thank you for your vote of confidence. To my daughter, Jorja, who sat beside me patiently watching cartoons while I finished *just one more chapter*. So much thanks to all those indie writers out there who allowed me to read their books for the purpose of writing this manual; I hope I have helped you as much as you have helped me. And again, to Blackbird LSD who took one of my crazy, midnight epiphanies and made it something bigger.

Introduction

Welcome to writing in the twenty-first century. If you are reading this, then you are considering publishing or writing a manuscript. Congratulations on this decision and may the literary world be on your side.

This book is intended for indie authors, self-published authors, novice authors, authors with multiple books to their name, editors, and beta readers. With that said, this book is not intended to replace a content editor, but instead to teach you some of what they know, and learn to identify errors in the future and fix them on your own. Only you will know if your work needs content editing, line editing, book doctoring, or a combination. The problem with that last statement is that many first time and newer authors feel compelled to not use the assistance of editors or even beta readers. There is an overwhelming notion that with a little bit of grammatical brushing-up, many errors can be fixed or might go unnoticed by the common reader. It's this critical error in judgment which holds back many talented writers from moving past the query stage when submitting their work. That may sound harsh, but it is the cold, hard truth. Every writer would like to think they've written the perfect manuscript, free of errors, but that's not likely to occur. As an editor once told me, "Look beyond your own pride, think of your readers."

This book is intended for novice and skilled writers alike, as we always have something new to learn or explore. Don't be mistaken as this is not a grammar 101 book. If you feel the need to refuel your grammar skills, then there are plenty of online community college classes, as well as helpful books on the shelves, or resources spanning the World Wide Web. But I warn you again, unless you are a skilled grammatical editor, do not rely solely on your own knowledge. And, even if you are a skilled editor or adorned with a well-deserved MFA, it's still wise to have another set of eyes reviewing your work, since we tend to read words that are not there because we already know what a sentence *should* say, not what it actually *does* say.

What this book is expected to accomplish is to teach you about several errors beyond grammar written into the content, errors which make reading less exciting, things such as author intrusion, head-hopping, and foresight to name a few. It will also cover taking out repetition and avoiding some common pitfalls such as unnecessary product placement, over dramatization, and a twenty-first century take on backstories. These are common errors made by many new authors which may or might not go noticed by readers, but are usually caught by editors and agents. Make any one of these literary errors in the first chapter and an agent may never move beyond that, and your proposed bestseller is axed and tossed into the trash.

Writers beware! I said many of these errors may go unnoticed by readers, however today's readers are quite savvy. They seek meaning, symbolism, and a well thought out, first rate book. They get frustrated with stories that don't go anywhere, or have too much meaningless detail. They want to be part of the story, part of the character, and feel strongly involved. All of these elements will allow a reader to engage without feeling displaced from the story. What you don't want is your reader to be removed from what is going on by idle bantering to fill space. Readers can, and often do, catch when a writer has added storyline to fill space. If a story can be told in 120 pages don't stretch it to 220 with a bunch of meaningless filler. This is not to generalize every reader, but they are out there.

You may wonder how I'm qualified to be writing on this subject matter; the answer is easy. I am a connoisseur of indie books from many genres. I have been reading books from independent authors for years and have come across the same errors in countless books, from both new authors and writers claiming to have multiple books on the market. Errors that have caused me to skip over pages due to repetition (sometimes word for word), or have been filled with so much meaningless detail that I was upset when it led to nothing. I have critiqued and helped other authors improve their books or storylines from the research that took me months to find when writing my initial manuscript draft, but it wasn't until I put out my second book that I was face-to-face with an editor giving me the "naughty, rookie author" lecture, it was embarrassing, yet humbling and eye opening. It was definitely much easier to give advice than put it into action. This is when I learned, just because I have a story in my heart and down on paper doesn't mean I am without fault in the mechanics of the story.

I committed so many errors that I was advised to hire a book doctor who would rewrite my manuscript the correct way. Of course this kind of service does not come cheap, and I was already in debt with purchasing a publishing package from an assisted publishing house. I resolved to research and *doctor* my own manuscript. They said it couldn't be done or it would still have literary suicide errors, but they had never met me or known of my stubbornness and determination when someone tells me, "it can't be done." From that day on, I researched all the errors in my book, read every website I could find and purchased a few wordy books — which were far outdated. Countless hours were spent on the phone speaking with editors who would give me the time of day to answer my relentless questions. All of these lessons learned were jotted down on paper and brought together for this book, so you could learn from my mistakes.

Over one month later, I had completely rewritten my second book, *Be Still*. And by rewritten, I mean the entire book was overhauled with point of view maintained, symbolism inserted into correct areas, removal of duplicity, and taking out author intrusion and foresight. My rep told me he had never seen someone with no previous experience do such an amazing job at restructuring a work. I felt a twinge of pride well up, but more so because they said it couldn't be done. I love proving people wrong. Later that month, I was awarded with the Editor's Choice designation and a few months later given the Rising Star designation, both from the assisted publishing company I went through to put that book on the market. Not bad for a fresh author who was advised to purchase an outside professional service to do the hard work for me. And I reiterate, it was very hard, tedious work.

The point here is this: You can do it. Although I still recommend getting an editor as a second set of eyes, keep in mind that some editors are only looking for grammar and punctuation. It is your responsibility to know what your editor is looking for, but also to be able to find some errors and correct them yourself. A book doctor, as expensive if not more pricey than a traditional editor, will point out mistakes in the meat of the manuscript and fix them on your behalf. This kind of editing may lead to a complete overhaul of a manuscript, with some book doctors taking creative liberties as needed or allowed. Be mindful when allowing another person to overhaul your work, you may just lose some of your own creative voice in the process. No matter what route you take, it is imperative that you always reread the edited manuscript with a very close eye to detail. Editors aren't perfect, they miss the obvious too.

In this book, I will explain how you can be your own book doctor and content editor, to see mistakes and fix them, and eventually learn to catch them before they occur. Having the ability to catch mistakes before they happen will save time and money in the future. I have taken time to do all the painstaking hours of research so you don't have to. And, unlike some of the wordier and outdated books on this content, I have written it in a way that should make complete sense and will engage you to think about some of these topics. The ends of some chapters have resource websites which you can look into for more information. These websites are not endorsements or advertisements (with the exception of WritingApocalypse.com), but put there to lead you in the right direction.

Publishing is a business. Publishers dole out large sums of money to edit and re-edit, the less work they have to put into it the better your chances are in having them read your query, or in landing an agent to represent your manuscript. The less errors there are in your manuscript, the more you appear to take pride in your work, the more attractive your material may become.

By the way, that second book of mine went through three editing processes after the initial verbal assault, and it still has errors that were overlooked, yet caught by my readers. For that reason, I can't say enough that you must always reread the edited manuscript before turning it in for a final print up. You should be aware that many readers take pleasure in pointing out the negative, especially in public reviews. Not every reader will love your book, many reviews reflect negatively based on personal taste for the material written. What an author doesn't want is a negative review assaulting and viciously pointing out every content and mechanical mistake made. A review like that can make potential readers look elsewhere.

This book offers up assistance and advise that most content editors would give for a large fee. It is full of lessons I've learned the hard way, but did ultimately have to learn in order to raise the bar for myself and the reputation of independent authors. In order to write an effective storyline, you must first know what elements are effective and which should be eliminated in or after the first draft. Knowing these elements will lessen the amount of time spent in editing and will flow into future writings. Being knowledgeable is not only beneficial to you but also to the reader. Writing a book is a mutual relationship between the two, you write a book and a reader reads it. From that, a lifelong bond can be formed, or a parting of ways may occur.

Independent authors have received a lashing since conception, and much of this is due to the lack of discipline needed to publish a manuscript. Anybody can put pen to paper, and everybody does have a story in them, but not every person can write effectively. However, when one independent author puts out a poorly written work it can, and has, reflected adversely on other indie authors. It is imperative that anything intended to be published go through at least one editing process. There are hundreds of editors out there at reasonable prices, they simply need to be searched out. This book does not replace that editing process. This book serves to arm writers, independent editors, and beta readers with the tools needed to write or edit a cohesive manuscript, to bump up the bar a notch and give indie writers a shot on the market, and to compete in the literary world.

I encourage all authors, indie and mainstream, to make this vow:

> I realize having an editor is as important as writing my manuscript. My story deserves to not only be read, but my readers deserve to have a well written book. My name, and therefore my reputation, is attached to this book, which holds me accountable not only as an author, but an author who represents the proud group of self-published authors. As such, I will demand perfection in everything I produce and encourage other authors to do the same.

With the exception of my own book or works in progress, no other books have been quoted in this manual. Some books have been noted as examples for the section they relate to, however, I am in no way reimbursed or affiliated with these books, authors, or publishing houses. I may make reference to something I read or noticed, however no individual author is being singled out. This manual has been written after reading indie books for well over three years, as such, all the comments made are generalized and any examples given are purely from my imagination and not pulled from any other author's books.

This is an interactive book at times. You will need something to write with and a notepad, as some sections will have a writing exercise. Other sections will ask you to look at a copy of your own work or work in progress. It is not necessary to have anything written to proceed. This is a manual designed to be a reference guide for all levels of writers, including those waiting for their story to be written. Much of the information given on the pages to follow are geared toward the third person, limited point of view, which is the most common form of writing. Some exceptions are noted, and some information pertains to all viewpoints such as back story, use of all capitals, italics, and more.

This manual was given a thorough initial editing for the first draft. Since I do mention the use of beta readers in a later section, I thought it would only be fitting to use beta readers for the second and third drafts. This manual has gone through many changes since the first draft, including the addition of three more sections. See how my two beta readers (found through two different online groups) did with the final editing.

Section 1: Point of View
THE PERSON SPEAKING

What is point of view? This is the voice in which your story is being told.

In order to proceed with this book and start on the journey to being your own book doctor, it's necessary to first have a standing comprehension of point of view (POV), sometimes called view point. This is something many authors have a great deal of knowledge about, but sometimes confuse when actually starting the writing process. When choosing to start writing a book it should be clear in what POV the story will be told. This section isn't intended to cover every aspect of POV, that could encompass an entire book of its own, but rather intended to give a quick refresher. If you need more in-depth knowledge into POV there are several books available as well as a wealth of knowledge on the internet.

POV consists of first person, second person, third person, and alternating POV which can then be further broken down into third person omniscient, subjective, and objective. All of these POVs are collectively listed under the umbrella of *narrative voice*, which can be reliable or unreliable.

Sound confusing yet?

The narrative voice is how the story is told. Sit back and take a moment to think how your story will be told. Is it told from a character's view point, by telling about an experience from an outsider's viewpoint, or by reviewing journals or letters? This narrative viewpoint is important in setting up your story. Once you have picked a POV you should stay in it, at least within that scene. Some books do change POV from first person to third person perspective, a change like that is a delicate matter. Done correctly this can add drama to the book, take *The Poison Wood Bible*, by Barbara Kingsolver for example. Conversely, if this is poorly managed it will appear as if the author is having an identity crisis. There are exceptions which will be covered in Section 3.

Now that you have your narrative voice, it's crucial to decide which character's POV the story will be told in. First person POV is often used in memoirs where the words, "I," "my," "we," and "me" are used in the narrative. Don't confuse this with dialogue which is noted by quotation marks (" "). First person is the telling of the story through the personal eyes of the character, as if the character has personally written the book. Think of it as if you are telling a friend a story about what happened to you at the mall today.

Example of first person POV:

I went to the mall to look for that pink denim jacket hanging in the window the other day, but when I got to the store they didn't have my size.

The lady looked in the back but she said they were all out. **I** was so bummed. That jacket would have looked so good on **me**.

See how that story was told from a personal point of view? It was all about me and mine. It's what I call the "vanity story." This type of story is sometimes difficult to write because the story is limited to information only the narrative voice (character) can know. This is why first person is easy to use in memoirs or autobiographies; however, it is an acceptable form to use in a novel as long as you are aware of the limitations it will impose. Used effectively, this type of viewpoint can be very powerful.

In a book currently in the works, the story is told from the first person viewpoint. I chose this POV because the story seems to gather more depth and energy by staying inside the mind of my hero, Matt. By using this viewpoint it also keeps my secondary protagonist a mystery, and for the purpose of this book it is necessary to keep her a mystery for the plot twist. The narrative in this book is first person limited. Matt doesn't have the ability to read minds, therefore anything told can only be what he can see, touch, smell, think, or hear.

Example of first person limited:

Alien currency is exchanging hands right now, yet I could care less. All I want is my charge up. I want my next level because I love the thrill. I love the hunt. I love the kill. And love to see what my new power will be.

This is the first chapter where readers are instantly introduced to Matt through his own eyes. Notice all the,

"I's" and "my's?" This story is told straight from Matt's mouth as seen above. The story is telling what he thinks, sees, hears, and feels straight from his mouth. In this POV, I can't write about what is occurring behind him, because he can't know what is happening someplace he can't see. This storyline is solely limited to his perspective.

Second person viewpoint tends to be reserved for self-help books such as this one, where the reader is actively engaged in the writing. Second person can be noted by the words, "you," and "yours." I have thus far asked you questions and will ask you to participate in rewrites. By using the word "you," you are personally brought into the book, making you an active part of the story. This is often found in music where lyrics are directed toward *you*, in which it feels like the singer is singing directly to the listener. Second person can also drift into other POVs, or come in after a different POV to create a different feel in a story.

Example of first person POV shifting to second person POV:

Alien currency is exchanging hands right now, yet I could care less. All I want is my charge up. I want my next level because I love the thrill. I love the hunt. I love the kill. And love to see what my new power will be.

Ever play video games? Not those sissy games like Mario Brothers. I mean the hardcore gamer games: Modern Warfare, Battlefield, and Call of Duty. When you reach a certain level, or get that certain kill, you gear up with new toys, new weapons and move to the next level. That's what the Monitors do with us: for every win, we get leveled up.

The first six sentences are in first person, then it shifts to engage the reader and the reader suddenly becomes a character in the book. It has the feel of following side-by-side with the protagonist. It appears that when he runs, you run, and when he speaks he is looking right at you. If this is hard to follow then think of it in terms of cinematography: notice how the characters never look directly at the camera. When a character looks directly at the camera the audience member, you, becomes pulled into the movie as if you were a character. This is exactly what second person does in literature.

Notice in my paragraph that the story starts in Matt's perspective of first person then changes to second person to draw you in. Now you are part of the action and you have just been transformed into a character, because you were personally pulled into the book.

There are no true rules regarding this type of change. My advice: if switching point of view within an active scene, ensure the switch is smooth and not confusing to your readers. I used a change in paragraph to do this. I would not advise changing POV mid-paragraph, and then changing back to whatever POV you were in before. This is very confusing and changes the pace of the story.

Example of first person changing to second mid-paragraph:

I loved Beth like no man ever could. Thinking about her all day was something I couldn't help

but do. She was my muse. You know, the kind of
woman that embeds herself so deep in your soul,
she is practically ingrained on your DNA. That's
what Beth was to me: A permanent part of my
very being.

Do you see how that example switched mid-paragraph? Did the pace appear to change? Whether you knew
what was happening or not, it should have felt like something was different. A change like that can cause a reader
to stop to try and figure out what just happened. There
are several blogs and writer boards on the internet which
address this issue of POV hopping, and what strikes me
as sad, is that so many authors give bad advice. Some advice states, an author has all creative rights and can do
anything within their story, and nobody should tell him/
her otherwise. This saddens me because, as much as I feel
a writer should not keep their creativity under a basket, I
feel the reader should be considered when writing a story.
When writing, the narrative should not be confusing.

Third person is the most complex, though the most
widely used. The story is told from a character's POV
with use of words such as, "he/she," "his/hers," and
"theirs." With this viewpoint, it becomes necessary for
the author to use the narrative voice as a character to see
what the character's see without the use of the first person narrative. This, essentially, is a hear-say type of story.
The characters give you a story, and you write on their
behalf like a spokesperson of sorts.

The easiest way to achieve this is to close your eyes
and pretend to be a fortune teller who can see through
the eyes of others. The fortune teller should not say, "I
am standing by a lake with my friends," but rather tell

the story as she watches the host: "She is standing by a lake with her friends." Remember: in third person POV the use of the first person should be reserved to dialogue within quotation marks (active dialogue).

Example of third person POV:

Jack marched straight into **his** boss' office, pushing everything off the large desk and declaring, "**I** don't know who you think you are messing with, but **I** warn you ... come near my family again and **I** will kill you." **He** slammed his hand hard on the desk then stormed out.

As you can see, the first person use of the word "I" was reserved for active dialogue. Narration was clearly written in third person.

It is best to decide what perspective you will use in your book and stick to it. With writing, these rules tend to lean toward guidelines—which you will read in every section—some of the great classics have combined viewpoints in a story by switching from first person to third, or by adding second person with third as shown in the example of first person POV to second person POV. For more detailed information on points of view, it may be necessary to reference the internet or a book specific to view points.

Writing exercise:

Take out a pen and paper and change the following paragraph into first person then third person. Try not to read the rewrite examples until you have completed your own.

> You never did like me. You should have just run away like you said you would. To think things were starting to look up. Then you arrived and ruined it all.

First person rewrite example:

> I know you never liked me. I should have just runaway like I said I would. Things were starting to look up, then I arrived and ruined it all.

Third person rewrite example:

> She knew he never liked her. She should have just runaway like she said she would. Things were starting to look up, and then she arrived and ruined it all.

If you aren't sure which viewpoint to write from, try writing your first paragraph from all three then decide which feels the most natural and which one has the right feel. Sometimes one viewpoint can feel dry where another immediately enhances the emotion of the story. Whatever POV you decide to write in should feel natural and not forced.

The problem: deciding on a point of view.

The solution: try writing your first chapter from first and third person POV to see which feels better. Make sure the story flows easily and isn't forced. If it feels forced, try changing POV.

For more information or brush-ups on grammar try:
www.grammar.quickanddirtytips.com

For more examples on POV:
www.writingapocalypse.com

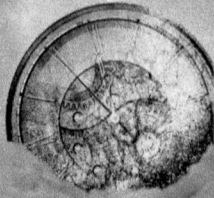

Section 2: Head-Hopping
WHOSE STORY IS IT ANYWAY?

What is head-hopping? This is where the author writes from the perspective of several of the characters within the same scene. Head-hopping is one form of author intrusion and should not be used as a general rule. There are exceptions to this rule which can be corrected with a scene break, covered later.

If writing errors could be classified as felonies and misdemeanors, then head-hopping would be at the top of the felony chart. It was my biggest dilemma and the error occupying most of my book, and the one seen in most self-published books. My novice author rational while writing was: I want my readers to be involved with and know what every character is thinking. Maybe you can relate to this sentiment.

As authors, it is imprinted in our DNA to want readers to know what the characters think, and experience what they feel. How limiting is it to only express the views of one character, especially if there are more key-note players in the book? What happens in this situation or type of thinking is that the author allows every character's thoughts to be displayed within a scene. This becomes confusing and is absolutely wrong and adequately dubbed, "head-hopping."

The first thing you need to know is what head hopping is and how to spot it. Once you can spot it then you can fix it. And once you can spot it and fix it, then you can keep it from ever occurring again.

It was said to me that head-hopping is the main reason a query is rejected. Why? Because, in order to fix this problem, the entire manuscript needs to be completely rewritten. This isn't an area where certain words can simply be added or removed. In many scenes, head-hopping is so overwhelming it's easier to do a complete rewrite, as I did — of an entire book. Something like that is exhausting and time consuming.

What head hopping does is allow a reader to jump between the thoughts of more than one character in a scene instead of staying with a key character. It takes away from the intimate relationship a reader should have with just one character, not allowing the reader to engage in every morsel of that character until the reader becomes the character and can empathize with the situation presented in the story.

Imagine this: a scene is written from three different perspectives over a span of three pages. It's not enough that the author change a few words here and there, sometimes the entire scene must be redone to stay within one character's head. This might sound easy; you will be given an opportunity to test your skills in a bit.

Example of head-hopping:

Jan wasn't sure what to think. She knew she wanted to be closer to him, to drown in the energy he possessed. Mike wanted nothing more than to leave, always staring at the exit sign, waiting for the moment he could escape. But Jan never saw this, she only saw the finest specimen of a man she ever laid eyes on and fantasized about how his full lips would feel pressed against hers.

This small paragraph is a prime example of head-hopping:

How can you spot this? Ask yourself this very easy question: who's telling the story? The first sentence would suggest we're in Jan's head, as it's Jan who's having thoughts about Mike. Move to the second sentence and we are still inside of Jan's head. We know what she's thinking and feeling and start to become connected to the character. All of a sudden Mike pops into the scene giving his own thoughts. We were forced out of Jan's perspective and into Mike's for one minute sentence. As a reader your mood should have shifted from a love struck woman to a man who is desperate to leave. The final sentence jumps back to the lust blinded Jan and we suddenly become a love struck girl again. Wow, what an emotional rollercoaster.

See if this breakdown makes more sense:

Jan wasn't sure what to think. (Jan's POV)

She knew she wanted to be closer to him, to drown in the energy he possessed. (Jan's POV)

Mike wanted nothing more than to leave, always staring at the exit sign, waiting for the moment he could escape. (Mike's POV)

But Jan never saw this, she only saw the finest specimen of a man she ever laid eyes on and fantasized about how his full lips would feel pressed against hers. (Jan's POV)

The question remains: who's telling the story? Is it lust-struck Jan, or anxious Mike? Now ask yourself this: was I able to completely connect with one character?

There is no saying who is telling the story since they are both telling it. Sure we know what they're both thinking which sounds promising, but it disengages a reader. More so, it can cause a publisher or agent to turn a blind eye to the rest of the story.

Another head-hopping example:

The diver took Jean by her soaked hand and helped her into the water. She was a fine specimen by his standards, the epitome of what a woman should look like. He was delighted to show her his world of aquatic beauty when he noticed a group of sea lions frolicking in the near distance. One of the male sea lions became jittery at their sight and began to herd his offspring away from the couple, not wanting his young to be hurt.

Question: who's telling the story? Is it the diver or the sea lion? This started out with the diver's perspective then we are suddenly thrust into the mind of the nearby sea lion. Do you see how your feelings are changed as a reader? Unless this book is told from the perspective of sea creatures, the thoughts and paranoia of a sea lion should never have entered the picture. First there's the emotion of the diver as he presumably desires this woman and wants to invite her into his world of diving, then enter the distrusting sea lion and all of a sudden we are herding sea lions away from possible danger. Wouldn't you have been happier staying within the mind of the diver? Ask yourself this question? If this is from the diver's perspective, how did he know this was a male sea lion?

Final example of head-hopping:

Steven detested his mother as he shot disdained glares her way. Evelyn wasn't bothered by her son's wild eyes and instead focused on Sarah who had brought up the taboo topic in the first place. It was like her daughter to bring up the wrong things at the wrong time. Yet Steven held no anger toward his sister. Sarah smirked at her wonderful upheaval. There was nothing better than seeing her mom exposed in front of the world. This was better than what she could have ever expected.

Are you as confused as I am? Who's telling the story? There are three characters here, each character is telling part of the story so the reader is never fully engulfed into one character. This makes for poor storytelling and also gives an omniscient feel. It's obvious the author knows all and has presented it which disengages readers, but most importantly it shows that the author is telling the story, not the characters. Do not fall into this trap if you are writing from a third person limited viewpoint.

The fix: if you have already written your story then the best fix is to reread the chapter and decide who has the strongest voice, then write solely from that character's perspective. It may be easier to ask yourself who has the most to lose or gain in the chapter. Once you have that answer, begin to write exclusively from that character's point of view. You can only write what he/she thinks, feels, senses, smells, touches, and tastes. You may not hop into the head of another character unless it is at a scene break.

What you *can* do is assume what another character is feeling. Let's revisit Jan and Mike and write entirely from Jan's perspective. Your task is to rewrite the paragraph only from Jan's perspective but allude to what Mike could be feeling or thinking. This is no different than what we do when we assume we know what someone is thinking. Do your rewrite before reading the rewrite example.

Here is the original paragraph:

Jan wasn't sure what to think. She knew she wanted to be closer to him, to drown in the energy he was drenched in. Mike wanted nothing more than to leave, always staring at the exit sign, waiting for the moment he could escape. But Jan never saw this, she only saw the finest specimen of a man she ever laid eyes on and fantasized about how his full lips would feel pressed against hers.

Rewrite example:

Jan wasn't sure what to think. It was clear to her that Mike wanted nothing more than to make a run for it. She noticed he kept a close vigil on the distant exit sign, but she only wanted to be closer to him. To drown in the energy he was drenched in. She didn't want to see anything beyond his being and was content to be ignorant to anything other than what she felt and desired. What she saw was the finest specimen of a man she ever laid eyes on, suddenly her thoughts slipped into how his full lips would feel pressed against hers.

Who is telling the story now? Jan is telling the story in this paragraph and we are able to make a deeper connection with her. Perhaps you sympathize or empathize with her situation, or perhaps you think she should snap out of her obvious fantasy. The point is, there should be a strong tie to the character and, if written well, it should be the tie the author is going for. Did your rewrite pinpoint who was telling the story?

Next, try writing the paragraph from Mike's point of view. You can make up whatever you want from what little was given, but you should have already been feeling something about this character. Is he an ex-boyfriend? Ex-lover? Ex-husband? Perhaps he's someone Jan's stalking. You can choose any storyline, but Mike should also be wary of Jan's thoughts without going into her perspective.

Rewrite example:

Mike was exhausted at listening to Jan ramble on. He couldn't help but eye the exit sign in the distance, like a small beacon of hope. There was nothing about this woman that peaked his interest, and the way she ogled his body was downright creepy. He resolved to call his friend later and chew him out for the worst blind date ever. The more he sat there, the more he felt all the energy drain from his body, he knew it was Jan who was lapping it up and drowning in it. She looked so smitten he decided she was lost somewhere in a fantasy.

Do you see how Mike can assume what she is thinking without leaving his point of view? We practice this in everyday life. You assume your boss is mad because you called out sick. You assume your wife will be volatile when she discovers you shrunk her favorite blouse. You assume your husband will be upset when you had the oil changed at some generic place rather than the dealership.

We all assume, and it's okay for your character to make an assumption about what the other character thinks or feels. However, it becomes a literary crime when you change the perspective of characters in the same scene. Stick to one person as a rule of thumb. Keep your rewrites of this example, you'll need them in the next chapter.

Now take the example with three character's POV and rewrite it from only perspective. Pick any one character, take any liberties, but all the same important details should be hit on.

Here is the original example:

Steven detested his mother as he shot disdained glares her way. Evelyn wasn't bothered by her son's wild eyes and instead focused on Sarah who had brought up the taboo topic in the first place. It was like her daughter to bring up the wrong things at the wrong time. Yet Steven held no anger toward his sister. Sarah smirked at her wonderful upheaval. There was nothing better than seeing her mom exposed in front of the world. This was better than what she could have ever expected.

Rewrite staying in one POV:

Steven detested his mother, shooting disdained glares her way as she eyeballed Sarah. It was always like his sister to go for the shock factor, but this subject was as taboo as it could get. He knew his mom was caught, and knew she wanted to wring Sarah's neck at the horrific news. There was nothing he could do but sit and watch as Sarah appeared to regale in the upheaval she caused. He was never mad at her, although he wished she would learn to pick better places and times than a crowded, swanky restaurant, but that was never her way. Sarah made it no secret that she hated her mother, and Steven sat back assuming his sister lapped up the joy of exposing his mother to the world.

Now that you have that down, rewrite the example from another point view. You should be able to acknowledge how telling the story from all three viewpoints changes the tone of the story. Each character should consume the reader into how the character feels. For Mike, the feeling is shock and disdain. For Evelyn, the feeling is shame and anger, and for Sarah, the feelings are pure joy and satisfaction. These sentiments need to consume the individual character so it can engulf the reader, allowing the reader to become the character who is telling this story.

One thing I will say throughout this book—in one form or another—is: writing is open to creativity, not an absolute. These are guidelines, though some points, such as maintaining POV within a continuous scene, have less of a gray area than others.

The problem: switching POV within a continuous scene.

The solution: decide which character has the most to lose or gain in the scene, stay within that character's POV.

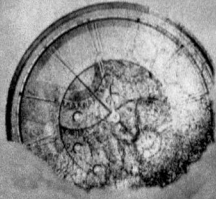

Section 3: Author Intrusion
WHO'S BEHIND THE CAMERA?

What is author intrusion? Author intrusion, simply put, is when an author breaks character and becomes visible in the story. This is usually seen when a character becomes omniscient when he/she wasn't previously, but can also be seen when the narrative voices becomes . . . well, narrative. It may be a matter of asking this question again: Who's telling the story?

Have you ever sat in a movie and been perfectly aware it was a movie? If the director did his job right, then the answer should be "no." As a viewer you should be so caught up in the movie that you are part of the story and forget there is a world around you. There aren't other moviegoers, no other seats, nothing except the story before you.

This is your job as the author of a book, to lead a reader so deeply into a story that the reader is unaware of anything except the story. Now let's say in a movie you suddenly see a boom mic at the top of the screen. Odds are, you will be taken out of the movie and you'll quickly say, "Oh yeah, this is a movie." The same occurs when you, as the author, make yourself visible within the book. This is what occurs during head-hopping, which is the reason head-hopping is classified as author intrusion.

With head-hopping it's a matter of deciphering which character is telling the story. With author intrusion it becomes a matter of, is any character telling the story? Many of us have been guilty of this without realization. We write detail, but no particular character is giving the detail, and all of a sudden we have a narrative deity speaking from who knows where. This may be acceptable in screenplays, but never in limited POV fiction.

Read the excerpt below and see if you can point out the author intrusion. Ask the question: who's giving the detail?

Example of author intrusion:

> Brandy was locked inside a dark closet. It was the worst form of punishment and the one she detested the most. Outside, the skies were as blue as brilliant sapphires. Not a cloud in sight. The hills could be seen far off in the distance while the scent of salt water filled the cool morning breeze. Brandy missed all of it, all she could do was close her eyes and pray it would all end soon.

The questions remain: who's telling the story and where is the author intruding? If Brandy is stuck inside a dark closet and the story is told from her perspective, then how does she know the skies are blue and there's salt water on the breeze? It's not possible unless previous paragraphs stated she was outside. For our sake, let's assume she has been in the closet overnight. In this case, the author has abandoned the POV of Brandy and intruded upon this scene, creating an omniscient feel. The reader is no longer sitting in a dark closet, being Brandy. The reader has been plucked from Brandy's perspective and put outside, then quickly placed back into a dark closet and the author has lost the momentum of what Brandy is feeling. For a moment in time, the reader is outside, experiencing a beautiful day, while Brandy is locked in a dark closet. The mood has now been changed.

This can be avoided by putting yourself in the character's shoes. Imagine being Brandy, stuck inside of a closet as a form of punishment. You can only write what she can see, hear, taste, touch, and think. If this is to be true, the part about what is happening outside must be removed so the author can remove herself from the scene. This isn't to say that Brandy couldn't imagine what the outside would look like.

Example of using imagination:

Brandy was locked inside a dark closet. It was the worst form of punishment and the one she detested the most. The thoughts of outside plagued her mind as she sat in that dark place. How she longed to escape, imagining the spring sky was clear without a cloud in sight. She pretended to see Bell Hill in the distance while she romped in the fresh salt water breeze. With a heavy sigh, she opened her eyes to darkness, realizing it was a cruel dream of a young girl. All she could do now was close her eyes and pray it would all end soon.

Do you see how we stayed with Brandy the entire paragraph? There should have been a different feel to the story this time. If written correctly, you should have felt sympathy for the girl as she pretended to be in a beautiful spring day. By staying with the character, an ambience and connection to the girl is built. In the first example we are never given the opportunity to reach this full potential of emotion.

Author intrusion is a violation into the world of your characters. Imagine the characters are arrogant and only want things to be told from their vantage point. There is no world beyond the world they immediately occupy. There are no senses beyond the senses they know. Stick with that thought process to avoid author intrusion. Occasionally, author intrusion is not as clear as with this example.

Example of unclear author intrusion:

The night sky was filled with stars. The moon was the largest it had been in years. In fact a news anchor had stated the last time the moon was this close to Earth was three decades ago. Andrew hadn't paid any attention to the moon or the stars in years. It had been the girls to keep his full attention since starting high school.

The author starts by describing a beautiful star filled night. Unless this is written in a third person omniscient POV, then Andrew cannot be describing the stars and moon, or the fun fact about the moon. The paragraph clearly states, "he hadn't paid any attention." Once again, the author has added details the character would have no knowledge about. The point is to stay in character, not veer into wordy detail like a commercial narrator. There are parameters restricting the author from intrusion to keep the flow of the story in sync with the character.

The best advice I was given was quite blunt: Get out of your own head.

Now, rewrite the above example, removing the author intrusion. If the night sky is not important to the scene, then remove it. If the night sky is important to creating ambience for the scene, then it must be described from the character's POV.

Rewrite, removing author intrusion:

The night sky was filled with stars. This was something Andrew hadn't looked at in years, as it quickly became girls to occupy his attention since the start of high school. But the moon was so large, so close, that he couldn't help but take notice of it and the twinkling stars. Kelly, the love of his life, sitting beneath his arm, mentioned that the moon hadn't been this close to Earth in three decades. How appropriate, he thought, that on a night like this, he would be cuddled up with the most perfect woman he ever met.

Remember the story from the previous chapter about love-struck Jan and Mike? Did you happen to catch the author intrusion in that example? Here it is again, in its original form, with author intrusion remaining.

Example with author intrusion:

Jan wasn't sure what to think. She knew she wanted to be closer to him, to drown in the energy he possessed. Mike wanted nothing more than to leave, always staring at the exit sign, waiting for the moment he could escape. But Jan never saw this, she only saw the finest specimen of a man she ever laid eyes on and fantasized about how his full lips would feel pressed against hers.

Did you catch the author intrusion? Even with this example having head-hopping, there remains the issue of the intrusion. If the reader can only know what either Jan or Mike knows, then how does Jan know what she never saw? The very last sentence clearly states, "But Jan *never saw this …*" Then how does she know if she didn't see it? If this story were written from Jan's perspective in the present, then she couldn't say that, because *she never saw it.* The author must remove this tidbit otherwise Jan has become an omniscient character. Do you see this now?

Go back to your original rewrite of this example; did your rewrite still have the author intrusion in it? If so, do another rewrite, this time remove the author intrusion.

One more point to make is on writing about a character. I know I previously stated that the characters are vain and want everything to be about them, but do not intrude on minor wordy details that describe them. This will make more sense in a bit.

After learning about different forms of author intrusion I wrote a blog titled, "Blue Eyes are Arrogant." This was one of my first blog posts, but received tons of traffic. I explained how writing the phrase, "He looked at her through twinkling, sapphire eyes," was author intrusion, and arrogance on the character's part. How?

Let's go back to only being able to see what the character sees, if I am writing in third person POV then the character is in fact stating that he looked at her through twinkling, sapphire eyes. But how did he know his eyes were twinkling? He didn't. He can't know this unless there was a mirror behind the woman he was speaking to. This is arrogance on the character's part and a sneaky form of author intrusion.

Do you see how subtle your intrusion on a story can be? You must always be aware of what the reader can see, hear, smell, touch, and taste. On the same note, you must also remember what they can't see, hear, smell, touch, and taste. Be your character at all times, and occasionally ask yourself this? How does the character know that?

The problem: giving details the character can't know about.

The solution: stay inside the character's head and get out of yours. Remember: the character can only see, hear, feel, touch, and taste the things he is aware of.

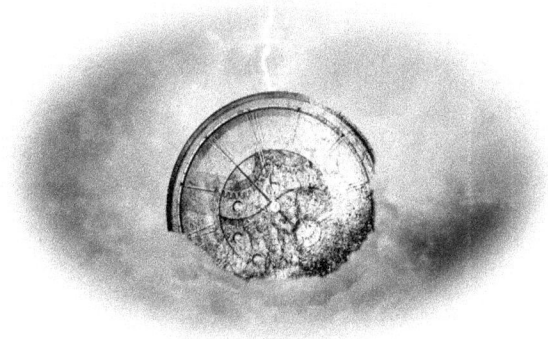

Section 4: Foresight
TELLING THE FUTURE TODAY

What is foresight? Foresight is the ability to see into the future, which most characters can't do. This is one of the biggest mistakes I have seen in indie books, and I was guilty of using it before my book make-over. Now if your character has the superpower of foresight then awesome, carry-on and disregard. This is usually not the case and becomes another literary crime under the heading of author intrusion.

How many times have you read an indie book that has this phrase, "He didn't know the bumpy road ahead?" Or, "she wasn't prepared for what happened next ..." There is a major flaw in these sentences: obviously the characters have no clue what is up ahead. In fact, it clearly states that in the phrases. These are examples of foresight, and can range from obvious to not so obvious. If this isn't clear then reread the section on POV. Recall, the character can't tell the future, but can only know, see, taste, touch, and smell what is before him.

The goal is to stay within the realm of the character. You must place yourself into the character and only see everything he sees. If this is done correctly, the character would not say, "I didn't know the bumpy road ahead." Stating that would be using foresight. It would be impossible for him to know what is ahead, let alone know there is a "bumpy" road ahead. Making this statement does several things to your book: it causes author intrusion, moves the reader out of what is currently happening, tells what is going to happen, and gives a cheesy cliffhanger.

Still unclear? Let's do a small exercise: Read the example below as if I were speaking to you in person.

All of this writing and explaining has made me parched. Hey, you wanna go grab a drink with me at the juice shop? I think you'd really like the fresh squeezed lemon-aid at the Juicer on Main St. It's my treat, wha'do ya say?

Now, imagine at the end of that last sentence I said, "Paula agreed to go to Juicers with me but had no idea that by making this decision her marriage would be on the rocks." Does that make any sense? It sounds like the making for a great cliffhanger, but in actuality it steps out of character, causes an author intrusion, removes the reader from the character, and adds a very omniscient feel.

This is how it reads to me whenever I see foresight in someone's book: there is a commercial on television and the actors are playing out the scene of a traffic collision. All of a sudden a booming voice comes in from nowhere and says, "Do you have Allstate?" This is exactly what it is like to read a phrase that includes foresight. The reader is in the viewpoint of the character, caught up in whatever drama is going on, and suddenly the narrator thunders in and says, "Cliff didn't know that danger lurked around the next corner!" Insert the dramatic some soap opera music.

The character telling the story wouldn't say, "I didn't know that danger lurked around the next corner," because he doesn't know there is danger lurking around the next corner. If you were walking down the road after leaving the Juicer would you be able to say that? Again, this is where a writer may imply or infer this, but it must be from the correct POV.

Example with foresight removed:

> After Paula left the Juicer, having the best fresh squeezed lemon-aid, she couldn't help but feel a shiver run down her spine. She stopped in place to look around, nothing was out of sorts, yet she sensed that danger was near. All of a sudden she realized she was very alone and danger could be lurking around any corner.

If it's necessary to say there's danger, then make it from the character's perspective. It keeps the reader in place and allows them to feel a sense of danger rather than being told there is danger. The reader should only experience what the character does. Foresight removes the reader from an active role into a watching, or passive, role.

Still unconvinced? Imagine this: you are sitting in a movie theater watching the latest horror movie. The woman walks out of the juice shop and remarks how that was the best lemon-aid she ever had. She's walking down the road, the camera zooms in on the trepidation she wears on her face as she stops to glance all around her. The camera pans across a desolate street and it becomes clear the woman is all alone in what appears to be a shady, scary situation. The music rises and we know something bad is going to happen as she takes another hesitant step forward. "What Paula doesn't know is that the hideous monster is waiting for her around the next corner," erupts from the speakers. I don't know about you, but that would be a horror movie buzz kill for me.

A movie is nothing more than a story set to film. As a movie wouldn't announce something is about to happen, neither should the author. Let the reader remain in suspense. Don't give away the future for a quick cliff-hanger effect.

This rule also holds true with a flashback unless it is in dialogue. *Be Still,* has several scenes where the protagonist goes back to revisit several memories. Here's where it gets tricky. If the character is reliving the past then it should be written without any foresight. This is to say, if the character is now telling a story as if it is just occurring then he could not know the future. However, if the character is merely telling a story of the past while remaining in the present, then it is okay to have foresight since he knows what happened. It is confusing, but needs to be mastered to be effective.

Example of reliving the past:

Corey put his gun down and cried when the call over the CB went out that the war was officially over. He looked at his blood soaked hands and hoped he would be able to live with horrific pictures ingrained into his weary mind. He hoped for a better future and prayed the love of his wife would see him through the hard times he knew would come when he arrived home.

Being in the present telling a story about the past:

It was such a difficult time, I explained. I remember putting my gun down and crying when the announcement over the CB said the war was officially over. There was blood on my hands, and I remember they were soaked and stained in this crimson liquid. There were so many horrific pictures of that war ingrained in my mind. My brain was downright weary from years of battle and years of losing friends: kids with guns. I saw so much death. I remember falling to my knees and hoping my wife would still love me. I didn't know then just how much her love would carry me after I arrived home. But that was a long time ago, and she still loves me that much to this day.

In reliving the past, the character is physically put back in time and telling the story as if it is occurring now. This is equivalent to a dream sequence, where in a dream everything is occurring as if it is in the present. Doing this now makes everything written as present, which means foresight cannot occur. In this kind of scenario the character cannot know what lies ahead, because in the present the future is not seen. This is one area that becomes very difficult to explain, but it needs to be said that the future must be kept out of the active past, as in a flashback or dream.

Repeat this, "I can't see the future if I am telling a story in present tense." Now say it three more times, go tell a friend, email it to yourself, and repeat it throughout the day. That's how serious this one is.

In the second scenario it's clear that Corey is in the present telling a story about the past, maybe to a friend, to a therapy group, or in a memoir. In this example, he's only giving a fragment of information about a time in his life some years ago, which means he's perfectly aware of what followed. Here, he knew the love of his wife would see him through the mental tragedies of war because he already lived it and moved passed it. In this case it's okay to know what would happen.

No, Corey's story isn't in quotations, yet it is stated in the first sentence that he "explained," which means he is using indirect dialogue, or speaking without direct use of a quote. In short, it is implied that he is speaking, and speaking about events that already had transpired. Notice the story is told in past tense then moves into the present. Again, this is indicative of knowing the past and every-thing up to the present. It would be wrong if the author intruded and wrote, "What he didn't know was his wife had just filed the divorce papers."

The only time something like that is allowed is if the story is written in an omniscient POV. But remember this: the story should not be written as limited with rare or spo-radic omniscient narratives. If your story is omniscient, it should be written that way throughout. If your storyline is written in a limited POV, then do not use foresight to add drama. Your story should progress into this drama. Don't give away the future, allow the reader to progress through the story allowing side the characters.

What about dialogue? Dialogue tends to be the all-around rule breaker, or get out of literary jail free card. Anything is possible in dialogue—even bad grammar.

Let's take a look at Corey's conversation again, in the situation where he's actually reliving the past, and see how it works with using foresight in direct dialogue.

Example of foresight in direct dialogue:

> Corey put his gun down and cried when the call over the CB went out that the war was officially over. He looked at his blood soaked hands and hoped he would be able to live with the horrific pictures ingrained into his weary mind. He hoped for a better future as he fell to the ground. Corporal Smith knelt beside him as Corey glanced up to see his friend's eyes were filled with bittersweet tears. "I know my wife is home right now, crying in front of the television," Corey said. "She's a good woman. A good wife. I know her love will get me through this."

Can her love get him through it? He couldn't possibly know since he hasn't lived it, but he sure can say it. He can say anything, it doesn't make it true, it merely makes it his honest thought at that time. I can say I know my kids will not put me in a nursing home when I'm older, it doesn't make it true, it only makes it my opinion at this time. What I would not say today is, "I didn't know a nursing home would be in my future." Why? Because, I can't predict the future. But for reference sake, let's assume I am in a nursing home and someone asks if I knew this is where I would end up. It would be okay to say, "When I was thirty-nine years old, I would never have known my kids would put me in a nursing home." In this case I am already in a nursing home so I know what happened.

Foresight isn't easy to grasp or understand with an easy explanation, except to say that your character can't predict the future. The best way to proceed is to once again step into character and ask, "am I in the past or only telling about it?" In the physical past would mean there is no foresight. If in the present, telling a quick story about the past, it's okay to have foresight, because it's not actually foresight, but first-hand knowledge.

Now remember your basic grammar, if you're talking about the past from today, it's written in past tense. However, speaking about something as if it's occurring now is present tense and equates to foresight not being allowed. Keep that in the back of your mind when thinking of using foresight.

The problem: adding narrative about events the character can't possibly know about.

The solution: stay in character. Stay in the correct time.

The problem: telling a story now about the past, versus going back to the past and telling a story as if it is just occurring.

The solution: in a flashback, everything the character talks about is a current event, meaning it is written in present tense and shouldn't have any foresight. If a character is in the present and telling about an event that occurred, then that event is written in past tense and the character can tell about how things turned out (only up to the present time), since the character would know that information.

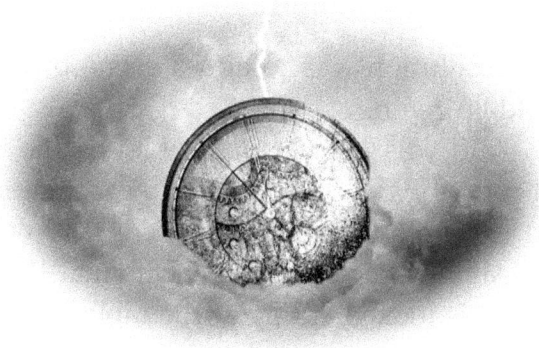

Section 5: Scene Breaks With POV
SWITCHING NARRATIVE VOICE

What is a scene break? This is where a break is noted on the page and goes into a different perspective, but it can also symbolize a change of POV, scenery, or time, so be wary how your scene break is being used.

In this section, I will discuss how to use a scene break for changing POV. Now, because every rule is meant to be broken — especially in *creative* writing — there will come a time when a scene will need to be written from two points of view, contrary to Section Three where I said to stay in one POV. Recall, I wrote that there are exceptions to the guidelines.This is where the scene break for change in POV comes in.

In *Be Still* there's a scene in a restaurant where Dr. Chris is airing a bunch of dirty laundry to Travis. I chose to write the first portion of this scene from Chris' point of view since she had the most to lose, however it is Travis who I wanted to really hone in on as far as emotional upheaval went. I felt that if I ended the scene with Dr. Chris, then the reader would not get the full emotional spectrum of what Travis went through when he heard the morbid news. The resolution was to add a scene break so both POVs could be given.

What I did was allow Dr. Chris to be the key character and point of view throughout the beginning of the scene and well into the end. She eventually walked out the door, leaving the reader with her final thoughts on how sad Travis looked sitting at the table all alone. She exits and I inserted a scene break, which is commonly noted by double spacing into the next paragraph. Now, I can start with Travis sitting at the table feeling somewhat despondent over what had just transpired. I can stay in his perspective so readers have the opportunity to jump into his head without taking away from the story, or head-hopping. This is an effective method but should be used sparingly as it can get confusing if over used within the same main scene or chapter repeatedly.

Example of a scene break for POV change:

The restaurant fell silent at the commotion and Chris immediately sank into her chair, feeling a lump forming thick in her throat. She never intended to betray her best friend. She only did what she felt was right and had to be said. Watching Jack walk out the door was as devastating as she had ever felt. Watching Travis sit there, across from her, she felt a sudden need to run out the door. He was pathetic: he sat there in his pristine suit, neck tie pulled up tight around his Adam's apple. She had nothing to say to him. Nothing more. Seconds later she found herself standing at the door, upset at the fact that she glanced back at Travis longer than intended. Suddenly, she didn't see some stuffy, pompous lawyer, but a man strangled at his own hands. She walked out before she started to feel sorrier for him.

Whispers began to grow into dull conversation around him. Travis knew the moment she walked out the door. He could feel the room begin to wake up and knew it was because of her absence. In a choking bit of courage, he glanced at the empty chairs around him. Taking in the night's conversation was more than he expected. There was something about Chris he wanted to hate, yet couldn't help but feel saddened at the secret she had to bear. And then there was the matter of his father; damn. Travis lowered his head until it slammed against the table. The pain left temporary comfort to the excruciating ache that felt like a vice on his brain.

The first paragraph is written purely from Chris' point of view. It tells how she feels and what she sees. Then there is a scene break noted by the double spacing between paragraphs and we move into Travis' point of view. This was important to my book because this chapter was a turning point, and it was crucial readers also knew what was going on in Travis' head. Originally, this was riddled with head-hopping, and I felt it was my opus in the story! Upon my editorial scolding, I completely rewrote six pages, all written only from Chris' POV, which ended when she walked out the door. After the second edit, the chapter didn't hold the emotion it should have. The missing piece was Travis. It was imperative to the scene that Travis' voice be heard, his emotions be felt. And so, rewrites three and four came forth until I understood scene breaks, then rewrite five emerged as my favorite and last rewrite of them all, complete with two viewpoints and a scene break.

The reason I relay my stories is so you can understand what I went through, and know you are not alone in this. Changing a chapter filled with head-hopping isn't an easy fix the first time, but it does get easier. Keep working at it, and know how to use your scene breaks.

The previous scene break example shows how to split one continuous scene into two different POVs. This can be done repeatedly within one main scene, but should be done with caution. This can be used when two people's perspectives go back and forth within a continuous scene. There is another scene in *Be Still* where the reader is following Travis' progression toward the hospital and Chris' time at the hospital. They are each watching the clock, thinking about the other, and pushing through their own anxiety. It was necessary to use several scene breaks within one chapter in order for this to be effective.

When using several scene breaks within one chapter, be sure that the scenes in between are full. This does not work well when only using small bits of dialogue or narrative and then scene breaking, it becomes confusing. The scenes in between should be concise and insure that the reader knows exactly whose head they are in. The scene shouldn't be vague and should state very early on whose POV we are. There's nothing worse than having to get through two paragraphs before realizing who the scene is about, then going into another scene break immediately after that, and again running through several paragraphs before knowing who the following scene is about.

A scene break is not a means to retell the same scene from different perspectives, unless that's exactly what your book is supposed to do, which would mimic an interview where several characters are grilled about the exact same topic as in Chuck Palahniuk's, *Rant*. This might do well in a crime novel, but not so much in general fiction unless the author has mastered how to smoothly make these transitions.

Some scene breaks are noted with asterisks or other special characters which signify there is a change. If your book is to be exclusively an ebook, then my suggestion would be to use a special character to signify the change. The reasoning is, with the different formatting it's not always easy to point out a scene break noted only by double spacing between paragraphs. Some people find special character marks representative of the book, such as a crescent moon (appropriate font size) for a book about werewolves, or leaves for a book about nature, or a rose for a romance novel. The symbolism can aesthetically enhance a book as well as note the scene break. When preparing a manuscript to be distributed solely as an ebook, then using a symbol may be the easiest way for a reader to identify a break.

~ ~ ~ ~

The tilde symbols above represent a break in the scene. This would be easily identified both in physical print and on an ereader. When creating a book simply for ereaders, be sure to double check the spacing margins on the final product as many programs shift characters to work with their particular format.

If using a break to show different viewpoints of the exact same scene, it may be easier to create separate chapters instead. The reason for this is, a break is used to flow through one main scene with different POVs and not to show several POVs about the exact same topic. For instance, three characters all witness a murder from different vantage points and all three testimonies are to be written about the exact same event. First: do not be repetitive. There's nothing worse than idle repetition to fill space. Second: make sure the reader is aware who this section is about within the first few sentences.

Repetition wares on readers. Find a creative way to say they gave the exact same accounts. However, if each one is telling something uniquely different then create chapters. Again, this is not an absolute rule but rather a guideline; refer to *Rant* by, Chuck Palahniuk to see his unique take on this. If you are not Palahniuk, then you can certainly use scene breaks, but be certain these breaks do not become confusing to the reader. It is imperative for you to remember that the audience does not always see things the way you do. It becomes your burden to make the reader see what is in your head. Multiple scene breaks may make sense in your mind, but to a reader it may be jumbled and take time to work through who's speaking.

The problem: creating an effective scene break to change POV

The solution: ensure the reader knows whose POV the scene is in early on. If the chapter contains multiple scene breaks, then make sure each individual scene carries weight. Do not simply write one paragraph followed by a scene break.

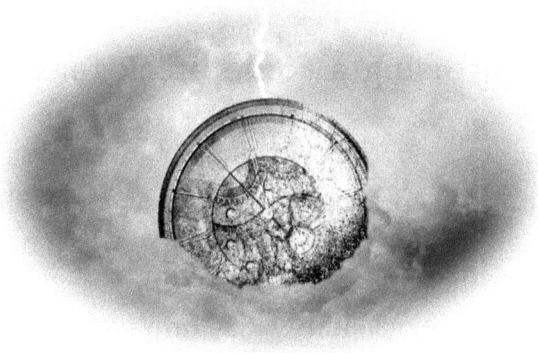

Section 6: Scene Breaks For Location/Time Change

STITCH IN TIME AND LOCATION

When else is a scene break used? Scene breaks are not specific to changes in POV only. They are used in flashbacks, flash-forwards, change in location, change in ideas, and sudden change in time.

The paragraphs following the scene break should have some meat to the change taking place, the same as in using a scene break to change POV. Meaning, do not simply write a few lines and then create a scene break. There should be substance to the story, and the change should be fluid. For example, if your character, Mr. Wilson, has a brief lapse into what he bought for dinner last week, then use narrative to explain this and do not go into a scene break if the flashback or thought only requires one paragraph. Too many breaks become confusing and overwhelming. On the other hand, if Mr. Wilson has left his cozy cottage in the woods and is now arriving in the big city without narrative explaining this, then a scene break can be used.

Example of using a scene break for change in location:

Jim Wilson locked the large wooden door to his small cottage home. It was time for a monthly trip into the city to pick up supplies: dog food, milk, bread, eggs, and water. Jim locked the yard gate struggling to keep Shep, the old wily terrier, behind it. The starting of the old Buick was usually indicative of a car ride for old Shep, but not trips into the city. All the noise had a way of spooking that mutt and left Jim chasing him around town. Not this time, he thought while kicking the gate with his heavy boot. With everything secured, he was ready for the drive into the city.

~ ~ ~ ~

Bridgeport was busting at the seams. Cars sped in every direction with a horn being honked at every traffic light. Jim detested these trips and hurried to run every errand in order to leave as soon as possible.

The scene break above was used to show a change in location. Jim Wilson started at his cottage home in the woods. There wasn't connecting narrative from his home to the drive into the city, so a scene break was used to show Jim was now in a different location. The break could have been avoided if the author continued the narrative marking Jim's drive from home and into the city, and kept a continual flow of action in the story. Note in this example a scene break visual was used, this gives the reader a visual cue that the story has somehow changed.

Example using active flow of events:

> With everything secured, he was ready for the drive into the city.
> Driving into the city wasn't a high point in his life. He hated the noise, the traffic, and the rudeness of people within city limits. He relished the serene drive while it lasted, the lush trees and greenery all around with the occasional sight of a cottontail hurrying into the foliage. This was as close to heaven as it got. But the foliage ended at the steel bridge, marking the entrance to Bridgeport. Beyond that, the trees were replaced with towering street lights and advertising boards. Short of a few weeds peeking from the road, the greenery was scarce.
> As he entered the city it was just as he recalled from previous trips. Bridgeport was busting at the seams. Cars sped in every direction with horns being honked at every traffic light …

In this example, the reader follows Jim's journey from home, through the woodsy highway, and eventually into the city. There's no sudden change of scene, therefore no break is needed. The reader is not jarred from one location to another without connecting narrative in between.

Using a scene break is solely at the discretion of the author, and often times lends to the writing style of an author. You can choose to have an abrupt change of scene with a scene break, or to carry on narrative from point A to point B. There wasn't a loss in translation in either example, the decision is based on the mood the author chooses to create.

In the one example, I used the scene break to show a change in location. As previously stated, a scene break is used to show a sudden change. These changes can also be in time and state of mind, and are used in the exact same way.

Example of a scene break in time:

Matt Gower had been at work for thirteen hours with no relief in sight. His eyes were heavy, mouth dry, and muscles feeling fatigued. There was nothing he wouldn't have given for some Ambien and a bed at that moment. Mila finally arrived, as he was closely reaching the breaking point, and told him to go home and sleep it off.

The sun was high in the sky when Matt opened his eyes. He wondered how he managed to sleep through all the noise around him: gardeners, busses, and barking dogs weren't enough to rouse him from the deep sleep he found in those early morning hours.

Take out a pen and paper and write that same story-line, but instead of a sudden break in time, write a story that flows through without an abrupt change. Do not peak ahead at the examples. Give this your best, creative genius and then compare notes.

Rewrite without scene break:

Matt Gower had been at work for thirteen hours with no relief in sight. His eyes were heavy, mouth dry, and muscles feeling fatigued. There was nothing he wouldn't have given for some Ambien and a bed at that moment. Mila finally arrived, as he was closely reaching the breaking point, and told him to go home and sleep it off. That was the best advice he had heard all day and hurried out to his car.

The car drive home seemed to lag, and he wondered if he had fallen asleep at the wheel while sitting at the red light on Tenth Avenue. No matter the case, he finally made it home. Without changing into pajamas, he pulled back the thick blankets and plopped his face onto the pillows. It felt like only minutes had passed when he opened his eyes to see the sun was already high in the sky …

How did we compare? There is no right or wrong, as stated prior, because everything in writing is a matter of opinion and perception. These are the guidelines set by the industry, but once you master these skills, you will begin to understand why they are important. For the end of this section's task, go read a book and see how others use scene breaks. Often times it is easier to see this first hand than to read small examples. Write down three scene breaks to keep for notes as future reference, or, as I did, flag these sections in the book with sticky tabs.

The problem: not knowing when to use a scene break.

The solution: when a storyline is suddenly moved to a different time, place, POV, or state of mind, then a scene break may be needed to show the reader there is a change. Keep this as a fluid movement, if the entire feel has changed then it may be time to start a new chapter.

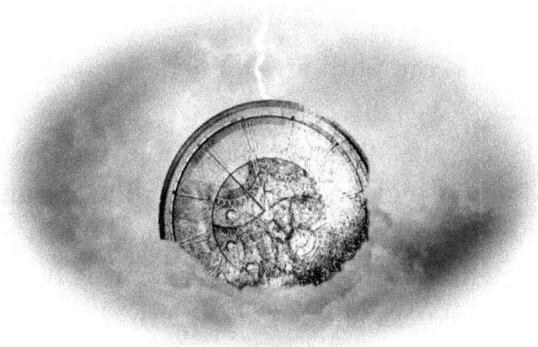

Section 7: Bold
TURN OFF THE FLASH

There comes a time when there's a word or phrase in which an author would like to put greater emphasis on, using bold lettering to make this statement is an absolute no-no and often times an obvious rookie mistake. Go back and read your favorite novels and see how many times bold reared its ugly, over emphasized head. Odds are it never did, so why does it seem to pop up in countless self-published books?

Your job is to make a statement using the written word as emphasis, not to bold the word or phrase. This is considered cheating, or shortcutting, and is aesthetically unappealing in fiction and non-fiction. Go back to the thought of watching a movie, since movies are stories put to film. In movies, the director does not say "I want that word emphasized so make the actor do a dance when he says it." Nor does the screen flash with a white booming light. The actor doesn't stop and say, "I›m emphasizing this word." It's the job of the director and actor to put emphasis on the word without making a huge flashy production over it. In this same way, it's the author's job to make it stand out without all the bells and whistles that bold lettering gives off.

Words are an author's tool of the trade, when used effectively the use of bold lettering will not—and should not—be necessary. This will take practice if you have become accustomed to highlighting words however, this is not impossible. Practice makes perfect and you're well on your way.

Example:

Red was the biggest bully of them all. Even nature **feared** Red.

The emphasis is on "feared," as the author wants to make it undisputable that even nature feared Red. Notice how the eyes are immediately drawn to this bolded word. Eyes naturally gravitate to things out of the ordinary. In this example there isn't much detail about why Red is feared, and so I chose to bold the word to make a poignant statement. Again, it's your absolute job to use your words well enough to allude to the fact that Red is "feared," without using bold lettering.

Example eliminating the use of bold:

Red was the biggest bully of them all. He taunted and tortured for fun. His voice was loud and boomed, banging like wild drums on a death march. His eyes were menacing with the rage and fury of a shark preying on unknowing victims. No kid dared cross him at the thought of being plummeted under his thick, heavy, swift fist. I was no different. We watched as he walked out the front door, even the trees seemed to hush. The birds stopped circling and singing, as if nature also feared Red.

The use of bold lettering on "feared" is now unnecessary. The sentences before the word made it clear that Red was feared. I hope I did my job by describing just how menacing this child is. Before, by using bold lettering, the sentences prior are lost, becoming understated to the bolded word. In short, the use of bold wiped away the build-up prior to the word, and all the reader sees now is one word. The bolded word essentially makes every other word bow down before it and become lost.

Bold lettering stands out on a page much like a black sheep stands out the day after a snow storm on an iceberg. The eyes are drawn to things that stand out in a crowd. If there was a room full of girls in bikinis, then the girl in a turtleneck and snow boots would stand out. If there was a room full of girls in turtlenecks and snow boots, then the girl wearing a bikini would stand out. Conversely, in a room full of men wearing three piece suits, the man wearing flip flops and a Hawaiian shirt with cargo shorts would stand out. When one wants to draw attention in a crowd, the best way is to stand out from the crowd. These are living examples of bold.

Now take a page full of typeface words in Times New Roman script and size 12 font and place one bold word on the page. The eyes are drawn to the change and the mind starts wondering what's so important? Some readers (like me) read so fast to get to that word, that they no longer relish the words leading up to it. In my case, I desperately need to see why that word is so darn important that it's highlighted.

Reserve the use of bold lettering for pamphlets or informational flyers. It's perfectly acceptable to use bold lettering in such notices when a word is noteworthy and to be remembered. Such as dial **4444** in the event of a fire, written in a new hire packet of important information. The "4444" is highlighted because that *is* a key number that should be embedded into the readers mind. It's necessary for it to stand out; in fact it can be a matter of life and death. The rules of fiction don't necessarily mimic the rules outside of it. Don't read how-to manuals on T.V. repair as a guideline for writing fiction or non-fiction.

Have mainstream authors broken this rule? Yes, look at *House of Leaves*, by Mark Z. Danielewski. In that book, nearly every literary rule has been broken, and yet it works. What sets that book apart is that the book in its entirety is a rule breaker. The author did not suddenly include a bolded word, or start writing sideways all of a sudden, but instead used the breaking of rules as a continuing theme throughout. Not many fresh, independent authors can get away with such genius, but remember this: these are guidelines that every author should have at least a basic grasp on when entering the world of literature writing, but it is still called creative writing for a reason.

The problem: using bold to put emphasis on a word

The solution: stick to using detail and description to put stress on a word or phrase. Words are a writer's tool, leave bold flashes of color to artists.

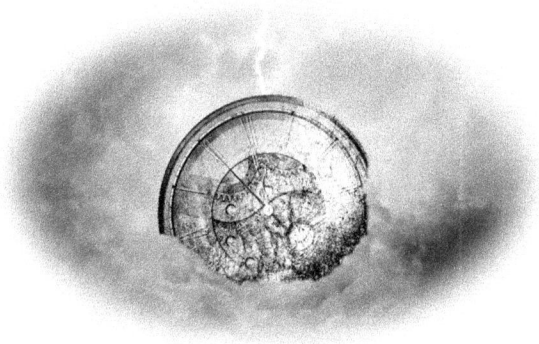

Section 8: All Capitals
STOP YELLING

Using all capital lettering works in the same way as using bold lettering, but gives a feel of being yelled at. Ever receive a text message in all capitals? Did it give you the feel of being shouted at or a sense of urgency in the message? This is the same reason author's place capitalized words into a story, to give off a sense of urgency, energy, or strength. IT'S WRONG. See what I did there?

IT'S WRONG. Does this feel like being scolded or severely warned? Did it make you mentally step back? This is an over emphasized statement which makes a reader retreat. It should not be the intention of the author to make a reader curl up into the fetal position and feel scolded or yelled at. The use of all capital letters is what's put on placards to warn people of danger ahead: DO NOT ENTER. DEAD END. CARCINOGOUS MATERIALS. MAY CAUSE DEATH. See the urgency?

It's wrong! The emphasis here is noted by an exclamation mark and makes the entire sentence have authority without being over stated by capital letters. The English language has given us some wonderful tools to work with such as exclamation marks, use them. It's a double felony to use both capitals and an exclamation mark in conjunction. IT IS WRONG! And, it hurts my eyes. The worse offense is to use bold, capitals, and an exclamation mark: **IT IS WRONG!**

Imagine looking at ten pages of Cambria script in 12 font and all of a sudden on the next page way at the bottom there are bold capital letters with an exclamation. Ask yourself this: Would I see every other word or just those highlighted ones? Would I still read at the same pace, or faster to find out what is so important? Would my eyes continually wander down at the bolded words? Would I cheat and read the highlighted words before starting at the top of the page? When I saw the bold on previous pages were my eyes instantly drawn to it?

Words written in all capitals also stand out on a page. The human mind is trained to catch changes in pattern and become drawn to it. It cannot be expressed enough that you are telling a story with words. Use your vast dictionary of words to let a reader know how important the subject is. Use words to give depth and help the reader understand what is so important without blaring out a visual cue. Visual is for art. Words are for books. Be mindful of which you are trying to accomplish.

As authors, we are expected to be able to write emotion into context. We should be able to use language to express what characters are feeling. Do not take the easy route by substituting quality writing with words written in all bold or capital letters. These types of errors are quickly picked up by agents. And it is these types of errors that show the big shots just how uneducated in the world of publishing a new author can be. No author wants to be rejected based on simple lettering issues. The best advice I was given by an editor on this subject is this: Until the day you are Palahniuk, Patterson, or Rice, you must follow all the rules laid out by the powers that be, unless what you have is truly ingenious and stands apart from everything else on the shelves.

Does your work make a bold statement? Chances are, though you may have a great story, the story will not change the face of literature. There are always exceptions, but where I say don't underestimate yourself, I must also say don't overestimate yourself. Know when it's okay to break the rules, and when it's necessary to follow the standard.

Is all capital lettering ever okay? In the twenty-first century, with digital media taking over, scenes with texting often times use capital lettering to voice who is speaking. One industry standard states it is acceptable to use all capital lettering when declaring who is sending a message. Sometimes this decision is based upon who is proofing the manuscript, as several editors have given me several different answers to this question. One thing is certain: this is not an absolute rule as of yet, and to date I continue to use the capitalization of the first name only when showing who is sending a message. The style is yours alone.

Example of all capital lettering in a text message:

LYNN: *Boo hoo. You whine too much*

GRANT: *I can't help the way I feel. LOL.*

LYNN: *Would you like some whine with your cheese?*

GRANT: *There's cheese?*

LYNN: *LOL. Always thinking of food.*

The problem: using all capital letters in the content of a story.

The solution: unless writing to show what a placard or sign read, or to show who is speaking in a digital message, refrain from using all capitalization to make a word or phrase within the narrative standout.

This is a fun site that answers the question: what do all capital letters typically refer to in writing? You will find most the answers point to the fact that it means someone is shouting. Note this site is where people can ask and answer questions and doesn't necessarily make it a fact.

For more information visit this website
http://english.stackexchange.com/questions/8672/
what-do-all-capital-letters-typically-refer-to-in-writing

Section 9: Italics (tone)
ADDING TONE TO VOICE

What are italics? Italics are used to separate a word or words from those around them in order to allow the reader to detect a brief change.

This section on using italics is an appropriate transition from the previous sections on bold lettering and capitalized words. Often times the use of bold or all capital letters can be averted by using italics. This is not the rule or the absolute answer to emphasizing a word or phrase, but often times a satisfactory solution when not wanting to get wordy, or if adding more detail would take away from the narrative. The use of italics is to give a reader a visual cue that something has changed, and help with the comprehension of the selected passage in the story. There are many uses for italics: when a person is thinking, to make a word stand out, to infer sarcasm, to name a book, for foreign words and other items covered in the next section.

In fiction as in non-fiction, the narrative states the emotions of the character. It tells all five senses, but what happens when an active thought is added? The author can state something like, "he wondered what on earth was going on." That statement is passive and written in a third person narrative. The act of the author *telling* a reader what the character is thinking is considered passive. When a character is in a passive thought the use of italic lettering is unnecessary. But what if the author wants the character to have an active thought? When the author wants an active thought (reader actively being inside the character's mind) to be shown, the use of italics is incorporated.

Example of a passive thought:

Jimmy stepped out of his house to find an alien ship hovering overhead. People were running and screaming from every direction. He wondered what on earth was going on then ran inside to check on his newborn son.

Example of an active thought:

Jimmy stepped out of his house to find an alien ship hovering overhead. People were running and screaming from every direction. *What on earth is going on?* With jaw dropped, he ran inside to check on his newborn son.

These examples show the use of passive and active thought. In the first example, the reader is told what Jimmy thought, this is called a passive narration or passive voice. In the second example, the use of italics puts the readers inside Jimmy's head as if they were actively thinking it with Jimmy, this is active narration, or an active voice. The italics let readers know there's a change occurring that's noteworthy. In this case it's Jimmy's thoughts that are noteworthy.

Italics can also be used to note different inflections in a character's voice. In audible language much of what's said can be given a different meaning purely through the pitch change in one's voice. In American Sign Language, the change in tone, or emotion, is shown on the signer's face. Or as I tell my kids, "Don't look at me in that tone of voice." The best audible example is a scene in the movie *Baseketball*, directed by David Zucker, where two actors are talking to each other using only the word, "dude." They go back and forth, running the gamut of emotions from anger to questioning, to apology and resolution all with a single word. Now try to put that into writing.

Ways to show a change in tone is expressed in different ways through language. In writing, italicized words are used to make something sound urgent, humorous, or sarcastic. The burden of inflection and pitch falls on the writer, but there are tools stored in a writer's arsenal, italics are one such tool. To put emphasis, a word can be placed in italics both in dialogue and in narrative. Your role is to not rely solely on this use or use it as a crutch. Using too much italic lettering can give the impression you aren't using your words effectively. Use italics sparingly and only when needing to point out a change in pitch when used within dialogue.

Example without italics:

Kevin had never been so mad at her. With hands in the air he shouted, "Do you hear me? You ruined everything. You ruin everything."

Example using italics as emphasis:

Kevin had never been so mad at her. With hands in the air he shouted, "Do you hear me? You ruined everything. *You* ruined everything."

The italicized "you" puts an emphasis on the word. If read properly it should have drawn out the word "you." In this example, using italics rather than bold lettering or all capital lettering is a good exchange. The italicized word in this case doesn't show urgency or give off the impression of shouting. It lets the reader know there's only a change in tone on the word. Most readers are savvy enough to pick up what kind of pitch is being portrayed.

Try this one: are you loving this book so far? Or are you *love* loving this book so far?

Using italicized words in narrative is a bit different. An italicized word reflects change in narrative tone and is emphasized by the tone preceding it. This is to say if the tone is eerie, then the italicized word would be oober eerie. If the tone is romantic, then the italicized word would be romantically amped. Do not use italics to change the tone of the story on a dime. But, as stated throughout this manual, there are exceptions, which will be shown later.

Example of italics to show emphasis on a word:

The child was without an end to her energy. Ally was exhausted at the girl's nonstop running and talking. Through the room, the girl ran and talked then ran some more and stopped to talk some more followed by *more* fast paced running.

The italicized word should give a sense of Ally's exhaustion since the tempo was already set up that way.

Example of italics to show emphasis on a word:

Everything about Marcus was deplorable. Kristen cringed at the very sight of him, at his toothy, arrogant smile, at the way he demanded attention. Watching him stand there, the epitome of a conceded man, made her skin crawl. There was no doubt she hated him, and *everything* about him.

The emphasis is on "everything." Again, if written with the correct tone, the "everything" should be read with a disdained sarcasm. The italics in the narrative follow the tone or pace set up. Its only job is to add that little pitch of human inflection into the current tone. It can be used to emphasize any mood: hate, disgust, energy, exhaustion, love, or fear to name a few. Some authors use italics to show an entry in a journal or a letter, to show there's a different voice being used throughout the book, or to show where examples are. If the entry is paragraph sized then this is okay use, however, if it's longer than a paragraph, the use of an indented paragraph with a scene break before and after works better on the reader's eyes.

With new technology entering literature, such as a text message or an online conversation, the use of italics has been used to convey the message after the character's name. No official rules have been thrown up about this, but if the author feels the need to separate the digital conversation from the narrative it can be done several ways:

Example of italics as text messages:

Lena glanced down at her phone. It was a text from Scott.

Scott: *Please call me. Please*

Lena text back: *Just leave me alone.*

Scott: *I know I'm a jerk. Can we talk?*

Lena: *No.*

She closed her phone and tucked it deep in her purse.

This can also be written in standard font, or with an indentation prior to their names. Including the use of modern technology, such as texting and chatting across an online chat room, poses new obstacles for the modern writer. This is where many other books become outdated, and where a new standard must be put into effect to reflect the changing times. After speaking with several editors, I was told there is not a specific guideline to adding a text message or online chat into a story (as previously stated), the above examples are what was suggested. It was also suggested, the writer should keep the text message or chat as simple as possible within the context of the story, and the conversation should stand apart so readers are aware there is a change.

The problem: misusing italics.

The solution: use italics sparingly where you want a word to change the inflection. When stuck on whether to use bold lettering or all capitals to make a word standout, opt for italics. When writing a paragraph in italics but wanting a word or phrase to stand out, change the word or phrase to standard script and font. Using this technique then makes the standard font stand out from the italics and is read as showing a change or inflection in tone.

Section 10: Italics (other)
OTHER USES

Italics don't tend to rear up much in fiction other than depicting a change of tone, but it does have other uses which sometimes work their way into fictional literature. As previously mentioned (and not all inclusive) there are: reciting major works, foreign words, when naming ships or aircraft, and when singling out a word for an example.

Italics in naming aircraft and ships:

- *The USS Arizona* is considered a graveyard and memorial site.

- Montgomery slammed a bottle of champagne against the ship's hull and dubbed her, *The Betty Ross.*

- Quiko, the dominant alien, said the aircraft was named *Belizario.*

- Yes, even the *USS Enterprise* is italicized.

- Italics in reciting major works:

- Jen recalled reading Tennessee Williams' *The Glass Menagerie* in high school.

We always knew we could find dad sitting at the breakfast table with the Sunday edition of *The Desert Daily* in hand.

Italics in foreign words:

- Walking down the street gave her the distinct feeling of *déjà vu*.

- Jose had a wonderful way of rolling his "R's" anytime he said the word *amor*.

Italics when singling out a word in an example:

- He used the word *ship* to represent an unidentified flying object in the picture.

- I was once told the class was named *algebra* because it was no longer math.

This section is a very concise example of when italicized words can be used. It may seem unimportant, but if citing a literary work and the wrong notation is used, it can procure several legal problems. Using italics in citing works or naming ships and aircraft is also a point learned in grade school, which most agents and/or publishers would expect an author to know about. Don't be terribly alarmed if this is a subject you need to revisit, many writers don't remember everything they learned in fifth grade. This is the reason there are resource guides and, in this technological day and age, there is no excuse to not be able to find at least one online outlet to study from. The World Wide Web has hundreds of websites to browse through, but this manual gives the most widely used uses of italicized words in fiction and non-fiction.

Things to remember are:

Every aircraft or ship, even alien or UFO, has an italicized name:

- *USS Kansas*

- The alien war craft, *Tamuka-5*

- My dad named the dingy, *Sweet Lynn* after my mom.

When singling out one word as an example, it should be italicized:

- *Italicized* is not a font style

- You say *bad* like it's a bad thing

Major literary works and periodicals are italicized:

- *The Los Angeles Times*

- *The Picture of Dorian Gray,* by Oscar Wilde

When writing a foreign word:

- *Mi amore*

- In Hawaiian, we say *mahalo*.

The problem: not knowing how to properly use italicized words

The solution: practice writing sentences. The more you practice the better you will be.

Now take out a piece of paper and write a sentence using an italicized word for each of the uses listed above. Try and write a full sentence. The more you practice, the closer to second nature it will become.

Here are the uses:
Aircraft or ship
Singling out one word
Major literary works or periodicals
Writing a foreign word

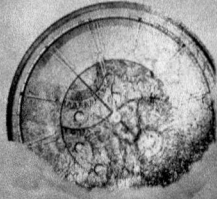

Section II: Repitition (content)
THE SAME OLD STORY, AGAIN

What is repetition? This is the notable recurrence of a word, phrase, or idea within a story.

If there's one thing that stands out more than others to a reader within the context of a book, it's repetition. Most people don't like hearing the same story twice, this also holds true to reading a book. The first time something is said, it should be said to the fullest effect and not repeated several times over the course of the story. A second option is to give small details and then give the concise story at the end. Repeating the same story is a redundant, quick, sure-fire way to have a reader scan ahead — or at least think about it. This also gives the sense that the author was trying to fill space. Don't lose a reader with repetition and/or redundancy.

In one book I read, the same story was told word for word several times. It was as if the author did a "copy and paste." To ensure I wasn't wrong, I copied the entry and compared it to some of the other places that it was listed in. There was no mistaking it: that entry was written verbatim more than four times. To make matters worse, that particular entry was three pages long and told by the exact same character each time. The only difference was in that the character told it to different people, and once in a different point of view. After the second time the passage reared its redundant head, I skipped ahead. Is that the kind of response you would want?

Repeating the story several times did not add to the story, instead it took away from it, and made me feel bored in an otherwise exciting story. Honestly, I wanted to stop reading after the third retelling. It became clear why indie books (as a whole) have been given a bad name. Not that this particular book was the awakening point, but it sure did hammer the nail into the coffin ... over, and over, and over again. It was painful. But, just to make sure I wasn't being overly harsh, I had a second person read it and told them nothing about the book. The outcome was exactly the same with one exception: after the third time the same story was told, the reader closed the book and never went back to it.

Since then, and since reading dozens of indie books after that one, the repetition theme continues to emerge. Can I throw stones? No. This was one area I was also dinged on when my book went to the editors. After speaking with several professionals, and doing some online research, I came up with a simple but effective way of keeping repetition out of my novel: a book diary.

A book diary is what many authors use to note key points of their story. It keeps timelines and details handy. Something I learned while writing my second book was that many things sounded familiar. My discovery was that some things came from my first book, since it was still fresh in my mind it sounded repetitive. Using the book diary allowed me to go back and find out when I had told a story and in which chapter. It's a kind of cheat sheet.

The other problem I found was that I constantly talk to myself. Okay, my characters talked to me and worked through their dialogue and scenes. I can find myself working through a scene almost anywhere: the car, watching a movie, gardening, playing with my pets. Sometimes, I went through a scene an entire day, trying to figure out what narrative or dialogue sounded best. The problem was, sometimes it was unclear if I thought something or actually wrote that something down. Short of rereading pages, it became confusing to decipher what was played in my head and what was written on paper, so it all sounded repetitive.

With these problems plaguing the artistic mind — and I hope it's not just me — it may become confusing for a writer to sort through ideas, such as what was said and what was actually written. One writer explained that she simply wanted to get her point across, which is why she repeated the same story more than once — verbatim. However, that same writer went back and reread the story and said repeating a story in the manuscript was boring upon reading it again. I then asked the author to read another book with many repetitious scenes, and the author said it was beginning to become clear how repetition can take away from the rest of the book.

To be an effective writer, ensure a dominant or important scene is written great the first time. It's all right to refer back to the scene in dialogue or narrative, but not to repeat it verbatim. Let's go back to the scenario of watching a movie: how excited would you be to hear a character retell a story five minutes long more than once? How about if the exact same five minute scene was shown more than once in a movie? Would your mind be taken away to wonder if you had seen it before? Would you wonder why the producer put the same scene in more than once? Would your thoughts be removed from that movie to think about these kinds of questions, even if only for a moment? Now imagine reading a book and reading the exact same story spanning a few paragraphs more than once. At some point would you be removed from the story to wonder if you had read that before? Would this be a major distraction? Would you begin to lose interest?

Repetition is not only boring, but it's jarring to a reader. The mind is a beautiful tool and is not only drawn to what stands out, but also to patterns. Repetition is nothing more than a pattern. However, in literature, this pattern stands out like that black sheep on a blanket of white snow.

There may come a time when a story needs to be retold in order to add something new. Perhaps something the character suddenly remembered, and at that point it is only necessary to add the new item. Don't repeat the entire story, instead only refer to the key moment just before or after this new item is to be introduced. The reader's mind will be refreshed and will keep them engaged. There are several ways to go about this task, and this is where you can show your voice and style.

Example of adding a new item to a previously told story:

There was something familiar about the house as he approached it, yet something seemed out of place. Cooper couldn't quite put his finger on it. This irked him, it was the place he called home for most his life after-all. Then it struck him: the day of the murder, when he walked up the cobblestone path, there had been a stone missing. He remembered his shoes became covered in mud and he was afraid his mom would yell at him for ruining a new pair of sneakers. Why couldn't he remember this three years ago?

Imagine, if you will, the day the murder occurred was told in fine detail a few chapters prior. Imagine Cooper had already told the story of the day he arrived home to find his mother brutally murdered in the kitchen, with every detail leading up to it. Would that entire event need to be retold here just to introduce a new element? The answer is a resounding "no." The only part repeated was that Cooper walked up the cobblestone path. It's there that the new element is added: there had been a stone missing, his shoes became muddy, and so on. This is used to recall an event and add something new and pertinent. Retelling the entire story is a waste of space, may bore the reader, and truly unnecessary to get the point across.

Beware: If this new information is not essential to the plot then don't add it. Your story does not need fluff or padding. The only thing worse than repetition, is adding a false sense of importance to the passage. The reader shouldn't read the last sentence of the last chapter and wonder why the missing cobblestone was so important, because it was never addressed anywhere else. Don't make a big deal out of it if it's not a big deal, this is misleading. It's also irritating and again lends to the sense of the author filling space. Read Section 15 for more information on inferring importance.

The above example is shown to explain how to fit in a new piece of a puzzle. Sometimes a character finds he has to explain something again, but no new evidence is added. In this scenario you merely need to infer the story was told again. Don't copy/paste the entire story to retell it.

Example of adding to a story already told:

The police arrived at her apartment and asked Kelly what happened exactly. Recalling the entire experience caused her to shudder, but she told them the story just as it had transpired only minutes before. She prayed to God she would never have to talk about it again.

In the above scene, the author has already described to the reader what happened to Kelly in previous paragraphs, but now a new character is asking what happened. It would be a travesty to the story to rewrite the entire event again. Instead, the author alludes to the fact that Kelly retold the story to the police. Not only does this keep the pace of the story, but it keeps the reader engaged and moving forward. Kelly may call a friend for support next, then her parents. The same rule applies: the original story does not need re-mentioning unless some new fact is going to be added. Let's say a week passes and Kelly suddenly recalls something about the break in at her house. She phones the police, but the original officer is not available so a new one is dispatched to her house where he asks her to tell him the story.

Example of adding in new information:

> Kelly sat at the table, wringing her fingers. There was nothing about that day she wanted to recall, or repeat for that matter, but she found herself retelling every gritty detail. This time she found a little more inner strength and managed to refrain from crying. She told the officer exactly how it all happened, except this time she included the detail about the burglar's scar. It was shaped like a crescent moon she recalled, running from the center of his bottom lip down to his rounded chin. The officer said a detail like that could certainly help the case.

This would be the third time she had to tell the story: once as it occurred, once to the original police officer, and now to the new officer. Do you see how retelling the story three times could be cumbersome on a reader? To keep your reader engaged, to keep the pace, and to move forward, all the author had to do was add in the new detail.

The problem: repetition.

The solution: stay focused and move forward when retelling an event. Only add in the new detail after telling the story the first time.

This is your assignment for this section: tell a good friend or family member something funny, exciting, or sad that happened during the week, but leave out a few small details. Retell the story again an hour later, this time add in a new detail. Continue to do this until you have retold the story the exact same way at least three times, but adding in a new detail each time. When you're done, ask your friend if they'll give an honest opinion of how they felt having to hear the same story over and over again. Ask yourself this: how did I feel about retelling the same exact story more than once to the same person? That may be how your readers feel.

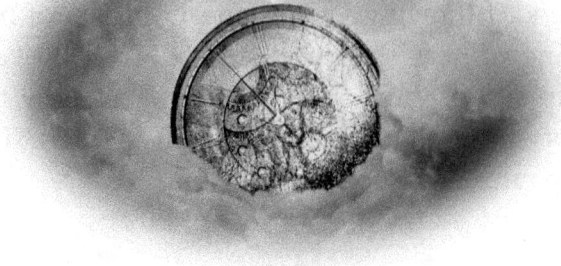

Section 12: Repitition (words)
WHAT'S A THESAURUS?

After years of people watching, I have learned many things; one is that most people have a catch phrase. This is a word or set of words that are used repeatedly and many times without the speaker's knowledge. We all know the typical words: "um" and "you know?" People say these words over and over without knowledge, but listeners pick up on them. This also occurs in writing and often without the author's awareness, since we don't tend to catch our own personal phrases. This is because they are so common to us that we have a tendency to read right passed them. However, content editors pick up these repetitive words and will point them out to you. Some words are repeated throughout a story, but spaced so far apart from each other that they are overlooked, but many are used so often and in such close proximity that a reader picks up on them—especially words that are flashy.

One book repeatedly used a flashy word like "melancholy." Most readers know what melancholy is so it shouldn't stand apart from other words, in theory, unless it's used repeatedly. In the manuscript the flashy word was used more than twenty-one times throughout nine-teen chapters. The author insisted the count had to be wrong, but after using the search function realized it was correct and made some changes. No, this word wasn't all that fancy that it stood out immediately, but after reading it two times within three paragraphs of each other, it became familiar and my eyes started to search it out. Each time it popped up, my brain left the story and thought, "Oh, there's that word again."

Example of repetition:

Elise was one of those persnickety women who looked down on everything and everyone. If her nose was raised any higher she would develop a kink in her tight neck. She walked around wearing white gloves, giving a disdained wince at the slightest hint of lint on them. Perfection was required and demanded of the staff and there were no second chances on a first offense. Hundreds of men and women had been hired only to be fired within the same day. One woman commented on Ms. Wayne's persnickety demeanor and it was rumored that woman can no longer find work within the county or it's bordering counties.

She was persnickety indeed.

What word stood out the most? Take a moment to honestly evaluate how reading the word "persnickety" three times made you feel? Did it distract you after the first time? How about when reading it a third time?

"Persnickety" is not a common word so it stands out. If it stood alone it would be a beautiful description of Elise Wayne, but when repeated, it loses its luster and eventually grows cumbersome and weary on the brain. The word becomes a major eyesore and a reader may begin to wonder about the ability of the author to use more effective words. Worse, a reader may be turned off and stop reading all together. Don't let repetition be a reason for a reader to disengage or leave a bad review pointing out this atrocity.

There are several easy ways to find these repetitive words in your document. One way is to go back and re-read what has been written, which I highly recommend. I do this after every chapter and continue to find repeated words. Another way is to use the search function in a Microsoft™ Word program. Most writing programs have the search function capabilities. By using this function, any word searched will be pulled up throughout the story. For example, if it feels like the word "tenacious" has been used a few times, then use the search option to find "tenacious." The function will point to every place the word has been used. If it was used in chapter one and again in chapter eighteen, odds are there isn't a problem to be fixed. If it's found in chapter one, four, six, ten, fifteen, and other chapters then it may be time to revisit a thesaurus.

For those who are unaware, the thesaurus is a tool which displays synonyms as well as antonyms for a specific word. This tool has saved my literary behind a time or two. There comes a point in the life of many writers when we get stuck on a word or lack of a better word. At such times the use of a thesaurus comes in handy, and nowadays this tool is readily available online as a quick reference. Using a thesaurus isn't cheating, it's using a tool of the trade.

Once, years back, I was writing detail about it being cold out in the snow, I referred back to cold, ice, and snow so many times it became boring even for me as a writer. A friend pointed it out and told me as an author I should have more talent than to repeat the word "cold" ten times. It was harsh but true, and so corrections were made with the help of my trusty thesaurus.

Example of repetition:

The fire rose up like a wild fiery beast three stories high. Jeff was no match for the flames but ran into it anyway. His baby was in that fire and that left him no choice but to run into it. There was fire everywhere: above, around, and below. The heat of the flames burned at his face, but he continued until he came to his son's room which hadn't been reached by the fire yet.

The word "fire" was used five times in the five sentences. The word "flames" was used twice within five sentences, and "fiery" which is close enough to "fire" was used once. How did you feel about this as a reader? Does it instill faith in the ability of the author to tell a detailed story using a spectrum of words? Does it make the author come off as incompetent? If the story of this fire were to continue another two pages, would you continue to read it? Would you become bored or start actively searching out the word?

These are questions you must ask yourself. And, to be truly effective, you must be honest with yourself. If it sounds confusing, lacks shine, or causes you to hesitate, then it's reasonable to assume a reader may feel the same.

If it doesn't sound correct then fix it, odds are you're correct about identifying a potential problem. You should be able to turn that paragraph into something colorful and engaging for the reader. Rather than sit and wrack your brain for a word similar to fire, save time and look it up. Also try to cross reference some of the synonyms suggested, you may be pleasantly surprised at what turns up.

Pen and notepad time again. Your task is to rewrite the above passage without using the word "fire" more than twice. You're allowed to take creative rights and make some changes, but try not to alter the story too much. Remember, don't look ahead. You have the tools to do this.

Rewrite using a thesaurus:

The fire rose up like a three story high red and orange smoky beast. Jeff was no match for the towering inferno, but ran in anyway. His baby was in that wild blaze which left him no choice but to rush in. The fire was everywhere: above, around, and below. The heat burnt his face, but he continued until he came to his son's room which hadn't yet been touched by the flames.

Does the rewritten version have more appeal? Does it keep you engaged? Notice the word "ran/run" was also used twice in the original version. To refrain from using it twice, and to make the paragraph more effective, it was removed in the third sentence and replaced with the word "rush." Using the new word added that much needed sense of urgency.

When in doubt, refer to a thesaurus; odds are there will be a vibrant new word to use. Also check your writing program to see if it has a built in thesaurus. Microsoft™ Word and Works programs have this capability, check your tool bar under the "review" tab then check the "proofing" table. Make sure the new word you pick is used in proper context. Using flashy words is okay on occasion, but you may run into new problems if using complex words too often. Know your audience before using the word "lexeme" instead of the word "word." Also, don't use a ten-letter word when a three-letter word will do.

The problem: repetition of words.

The solution: use the search function to find repeated words. Use the thesaurus function on Word to find a related word or use a thesaurus.

Reference website to visit:
www.Thesaurus.com (sign up for the word of the day to get a new word sent to your email box everyday)

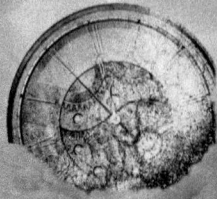

Section 13: Paragraph Format
HOW LONG IS TOO LONG

Is there such a thing as a paragraph that is too long? No. Again, this is creative writing, the difference is in style. What must first be known is that a paragraph is a group of similar collective sentences that deal with a single topic. When the similarity or thought changes, then a new paragraph is started.

Browse through a book, any book, and notice if the amount of narrative is a turn-off or turn-on. Many people sit at a bookstore, thumbing through random pages of a book and become turned-off at the sight of a page that's one excruciatingly long paragraph, or one that has too much dialogue. The problem I will cover in this section is the one of paragraph formatting.

Occupying half a page with a lengthy paragraph is not aesthetically pleasing, takes up a lot of space for one bundled thought, and with ereaders on the rise, one long paragraph may span three ereader pages or more. This is a new concept to consider when taking into account your book may be put into an ereader format. Can you imagine staring at this for three pages?

Example of long paragraph:

There was something in the way Mary answered the question that sounded more like sarcasm than wit. Brad continued to question her, but each time she snubbed him or gave a wicked, croaking sound to show her distaste at the line of questions. No answer was specific when she did manage to speak out loud, and Brad was at a loss on whether or not to continue on with his radio sow. By the tenth inquiry, and the tenth cheap answer, he plopped his head onto the table. Mary gave a little snicker, telling him his talk show was a joke. This peeked his interest and perked him right up as he pointed a finger accusing her of being a snobby priss. The onslaught of verbal insults was quickly tossed back and forth. Meanwhile, the yellow phone line lights began to flash with anxious fury. But Mary and Brad continued spitting the insults until they found themselves nearly nose-to-nose, seething like wild beasts. Mary cursed him for being a fool and a mockery of what the world now considered talent, screaming that he was no better than fungus feeding off the mucousy froth of other lower class animals. With that statement, Brad considered himself victorious in showing Mary's true character to a listening audience of thousands. Mary sunk into the back of her chair. He knew he had finally exposed her for the villainous thief and horrendous woman she was.

Odds are, you read that on an ereader. Is that appealing to look at? In the twenty-first century, it's necessary to now consider what formatting would look like in digital form. If you read this section on an ereader, then look back and count how many pages it spanned. Was it one long page? Did it span two pages? It may be one page long on a standard Ipad, but three pages long on a cellphone app.

There are many books out there geared toward authors that are similar to this one, many written in the early 1990's which do not cover the topic of ereader formatting. This has not been much of an issue since books were only out in physical print (trade back, hardcover) over the centuries, but a new dilemma has arisen since the dawn of the ereader: formatting for a smaller screen. Is this a real issue? Only you have the answer to that, but it is something you should at least consider when writing a lengthy paragraph.

The question remains: can a paragraph be too long? There is no right answer to this question although the topic has been brought up on many blog pages and chat rooms. The opinions appear to be divided. The question is then posed: should a book be revised between ereader and print books? That is a matter left to the author. What does standout among the voices is a paragraph should not be altered simply to fit an ereader. Some would speculate this is an area which shows the author's style and should not be tampered with despite the method of printing.

Ultimately, you have the final say in what your manuscript will look like across the vast span of physical books and digital capabilities. If a group of ideas needs to take up half a page, then that remains at your discretion. The important thing to keep in mind is that print is no longer the only option for reading a book these days.

Your assignment is to rewrite the example paragraph by making it two or more discernible paragraphs. Try not to alter too much, and do not add active dialogue (this will be shown in the next section). Remember: there is no right or wrong, only the author's style.

The problem: formatting paragraphs for more than one method of reading.

The solution: be aware that paragraphs printed in a physical book will look significantly different than the same paragraph in an ereader. Look at your manuscript across all the formats you will print in.

The problem: lengthy paragraphs.

The solution: ensure your paragraph is inclusive of only one main idea. Double to check to see if the paragraph can be broken up.

The problem: short paragraphs.

The solution: reread the paragraphs to see if smaller paragraphs can be combined into one paragraph.

Need a brush up on paragraphing:
Http://owl.english.purdue.edu/owl/resource/606/02/

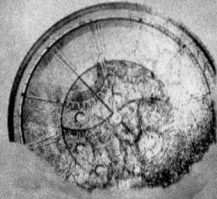

Section 14: Show & Tell
WHEN NARRATIVE SHOULD BE DIALOGUE

What is meant by "showing" and "telling?" Showing is when the author uses passive narrative to explain an idea while telling is an active means of giving an idea. Complicating? Don't worry this will all be explained in better detail. What needs to be mentioned is: it is imperative you be able to find a favorable medium area between the two, too much of one or the other throws off the balance of the story being told.

This section deliberately follows the previous: paragraph formatting. One way to break up a paragraph is to see whether or not there is a balance between passive and active narration. You should more over consider how much narrative is too much narrative, or how much dialogue (considered active narration) is too much. A well written novel should be able to balance narrative and dialogue to communicate effectively and engage readers. Refer back to the example written in the previous section:

Example of long paragraph:

There was something in the way Mary answered the question that sounded more like sarcasm than wit. Brad continued to question her, but each time she snubbed him or gave a wicked, croaking sound to show her distaste at the line of questions. No answer was specific when she did manage to speak out loud, and Brad was at a loss on whether or not to continue on with his radio sow. By the tenth inquiry, and the tenth cheap answer, he plopped his head onto the table. Mary gave a little snicker, telling him everything about his talk show was a joke. This peeked his interest and perked him right up as he pointed a finger at her accusing her of being a snobby priss. The onslaught of verbal insults was quickly tossed back and forth. Meanwhile, the yellow phone line lights began to flash with anxious fury. But Mary and Brad continued spitting the insults until they found themselves nearly nose-to-nose, seething like wild beasts. Mary cursed him for being a fool and a mockery of what the world now considered talent, screaming that he was no better than fungus feeding off the mucousy froth of other lower class animals. With that statement, Brad considered himself victorious in showing Mary's true character to a listening audience of thousands. Mary sunk into the back of her chair. He knew he had finally exposed her for the villainous thief and horrendous woman she was.

That is a very long paragraph, giving the effect of the narrator telling the action and not showing it since this is all passive narration. This is acceptable in small scenes, but in a scene with the amount of veracity such as this one, it might work better to *show* a reader and not *tell* a reader what's occurring.

Having difficulty distinguishing between the two? This is quite a difficult concept to wrap around for many new — and sometimes seasoned — authors.

Here is a real world type of example: imagine listening to an action-packed, fast-paced soccer game over the radio. The announcer gives a play-by-play of the game with so much enthusiasm you're on the edge of your seat. Players are scrambling, the ball gets loose, Perez snatches it up and kicks it long across the field to his teammate, and the announcer starts building up in excitement and frequency until he finally erupts in a boisterous and energetic, "Goooooooal!" This is an example of telling the action, the same as the previous passage was an example of *telling* about a heated event in Brad's radio studio.

Now turn on the television and watch a sports game. There's still narration from the announcer who is be able to see more than what's shown on your screen, but as a viewer you are engaged in the action before you, now you're seeing it rather than being told about it. That's showing. There is a vast difference.

In a power scene, such as the one about Brad's radio show, there should be a greater desire for the reader to be a part of the action, rather than passively listening to the action. This kind of narration is where the author needs to find the happy medium between *showing* and *telling*.

Example of limited passive narrative with active dialogue:

Mary answered with the kind of sarcasm which superseded wit. "You couldn't possibly comprehend the duties I attend."

Brad continued to question her, "What about the money you promised to the children's charities—"

She snubbed him with a bored guffaw which resounded as a wicked kind of groan. "They receive the stipend promised," she replied, followed by a yawn.

"And how much is that?"

But she gave no specific answer, stating "enough," then glanced away.

"Can you put a physical number to it?" he asked. She was content to glance at her perfectly manicured nails instead of answering. He continued with, "Is it the amount your husband promised in his will?"

There was still no answer. Brad took a deep breath, unsure whether to continue with the interview. He asked again but she continually refused a real answer and by the tenth time he plopped his head on the table with a heavy thud. Mary gave a little snicker, it was barely audible, but he could hear it.

"This is your entire fault, you know?" she whispered away from the microphone. "If you wouldn't have poked your grubby little head into my business, those charities would have received more than they are now—"

"The people have a right—"

"People have no rights to know my personal business, yet alone my financial endeavors. Men like you are rats on our society and your rancid talk show is deplorable to how much the lower class citizens are in need of a rat king. Any Rat King." she spat.

Brad leaned far over, poking an accusing finger into her chest. "You are the prissiest woman I have ever met. You hide behind money you never raised a finger to earn a day in your life, and you dare call me deplorable—"

They were nose-to-nose, ready to pounce as she hollered out, "You are nothing more than a fungus feeding off the mucousy froth of other lower class animals."

Look back at the original passage then at the altered passage, which looks more appealing? Which would you, as a reader, be more tempted to read if browsing through a book at the bookstore and came across that passage? This may be a matter of opinion or taste, yet it is noteworthy to learn how to move fluidly between showing and telling.

This isn't to say that narrative doesn't have a voice or should be turned into dialogue all the time. This is where technique comes into play. This is also where practice comes into effect. Most of the writing in a book is in narrative, or in telling. Telling is an important factor to give those intricate details within the story, the kind of facts which state what the sky appeared liked, the flower smelled like, or what the hero's brown eyes resembled. The key is to determine what should be told and what should be shown. Sometimes you must step outside of yourself and look in as a reader. If in question about a certain passage, look at it as if you're the reader. Is the passage something that does well as being told, or does the reader need to actively partake in the action?

Conversely, too much dialogue can become confusing and detour away from the emotion of narrative. When dialogue is over used the reader can feel like the third wheel in the conversation. It's like watching a tennis match, and the reader's head is bobbing back and forth without any other interaction. Where too much dialogue exists, a lack of necessary detail may also exist. Too much dialogue may also cause confusion, especially when the dialogue occurs between more than two characters. This statement can't be said enough, and should be engrained on the forefront of your thoughts: a happy medium must exist between showing and telling.

Example of showing without telling:

"You couldn't possibly comprehend the duties I attend," Mary answered.

"What about the money you promised to the children's charities—" Brad said.

"They receive the stipend promised," she replied.

"And how much is that?"

"Enough."

"Can you put a physical number to it?" he asked. "Is it the amount your husband promised in his will?"

"This is all your fault, you know?" She whispered. "If you wouldn't have poked your grubby little head into my business those charities would have received more than they are now —"

"The people have a right —"

"People have no right to know my personal business, yet alone my financial endeavors. Men like you are rats on our society, and your rancid talk show is deplorable to how much the lower class citizens are in need of a rat king. Any rat king." she spat.

"You are the prissiest woman I have ever met. You hide behind money you never raised a finger to earn a day in your life and you dare call me deplorable —"

"You are nothing more than a fungus feeding off the mucousy froth of other lower class animals."

Oh how the lack of some narrative can come off as exhausting. What if this active dialogue went on for another page? Bouncing between the conversation is fast-paced, and in this passage the reader is bouncing back and forth between bickering characters that have no suggesting personalities or emotion written in. This is like hearing a boring family member go on about an argument he had. "And then she said … And then he said … and then I said," and then somewhere in there the reader's mind wanders off onto doing laundry or gouging their eyes out.

Maintain a happy middle ground. If the passage is full of emotion, rage, love, anger, or anything else then decide if this is something the reader should be shown. If there is a passage about a car ride through the desert, then if would make sense that the scene be told about in a passive form. On the other hand, if there is a heated argument between characters regarding the real father of a baby, then it might give more weight to the story to have the scene be written in active narrative, or showing. A last option is to use passive narrative to tell about a quick remark, or minute dialogue.

Example using passive narrative for short dialogue remark:

Tabitha was bored with the conversation, she couldn't wait until her father's cellphone rang and she could make her lofty escape. There was nothing worse than being caught up in one of his long, political speeches about the sanctity of the American government. He went on for what felt like a million days. When he finally stopped to ask what her opinion was, she gave the answer he loved to hear, that she would vote for everything their family stood for so she could make him proud.

In that example there is obvious dialoguing going on in the very last sentence. This is an example of telling the readers what is going on. Using passive dialogue reads more like a play-by-play of the situation, where the reader is on the outside looking in. However, in this particular scene, it works well. The character is giving some insight into her life and the relationship with her father, but the small conversation doesn't require the reader to be shown this interaction through active dialogue. That is not to say that it couldn't be written that way and come across just as well.

Example of active narrative for a short dialogue remark:

Tabitha was bored with the conversation, she couldn't wait until her father's cellphone rang and she could make her lofty escape. There was nothing worse than being caught up in one of his long, political speeches about the sanctity of the American government. He went on for what felt like a million days. Finally, he stopped and asked, "What's your opinion, Honey?"

She knew just the words to say every time. "You know me, daddy. I only vote for the things that our family stands for. The things you taught me to stand for, because I love to make my family proud."

As you can see, the active dialogue works just as well as the passive. One thing to be observant of is what was happening before and what will happen after. If the paragraphs before were laden with heavy dialogue, then it may be a nice change of pace to use the passive dialogue and tell the reader what is happening rather than showing. If the paragraphs preceding and following this fill several pages with passive narrative, then a quick active dialogue might break up the monotony.

Ultimately, this is at the author's discretion—which can't be said enough. Again, this is where you must know your audience and have a firm grasp on your narrative voice. There is one book I read that had very little dialogue. My first opinion was that I would hate the book, assuming it was riddled with mindless detail but, to my surprise, it became one of my favorite books. The author made it clear this book was about a personal journey into finding the character's soul, as such, and as the character was primarily isolated from the rest of the world, it was clear not much dialogue would exist. In this particular book, the need to balance showing and telling was one sided, but it worked.

So much of writing is what you are willing to give, but you should be writing with a reader in mind as well as yourself, and with that, you should cater to the needs of your clients while feeling satisfied with the story she wrote.

The problem: balancing showing and telling.

The solution: add active narrative to strong scenes with dialogue, or to break up pages of passive narrative. Use passive narrative to explain dialogue which doesn't hold much weight, or to break up a passage with lots of active narrative.

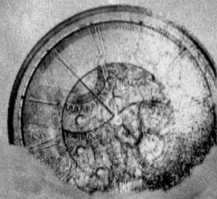

Section 15: Inferring Importance
WHAT WAS THIS ABOUT?

What is inferring importance? It is exactly what the question asks. Inferring importance is leading a reader into thinking something is essential to the story. This could be an idea, a physical object, or an action. When suggesting something is critical to the scene or plot, you should follow through by ensuring it is, not by leaving the suggestion of importance to be open ended.

This topic was covered briefly in Section Twelve, with the discussion of repetition. Recall the story of the man who suddenly remembered one cobblestone was missing in the yard. He remembered thinking his mother would be mad at him for tracking dirt into the house. This new detail should only be mentioned if there is depth behind it. Don't make the mistake of misjudging the readers of the twenty-first century, thinking they won't pick up on the hints you leave in these passages. If it's necessary to write about the missing cobblestone and go into detail about his thoughts, then this should play a bigger part in the story. Perhaps the missing cobblestone is a clue to find the murderer, or perhaps it was a warning left by the child's mother. Somewhere in the story the meaning behind the missing stone should be revealed. Otherwise the reader feels like a piece of the puzzle is still missing.

It has been said time and time again, every word in a novel should be necessary. If any word were taken away then the book would be drastically altered and lose meaning. In going back through the manuscript of my novel, I was challenged by an editor to remove anything that was not pertinent to the story. This was difficult to do at first, but after revising three chapters it became easy and those unneeded passages were easier to spot.

With practice, you will be able to find unnecessary passages. The best way to do this is to ask yourself, "Why is this important to the book?"

Example of inferring importance:

In Los Angeles, the streets are called "mean" for a reason. Children grow up fast. Drugs are found on every corner. It's a dog-eat-dog society where only the tough survive. Mikey was one of the toughest guys out there, with muscle from head to toe, and a pitbull attitude. He usually stopped in to buy chocolate milk every night, because chocolate milk was his favorite thing to drink after a long day of thugging on the streets. He was revered as "the man" within his small neighborhood.

What part(s) of that scene can be removed? Is there anything that doesn't add to the story? Is anything out of place? The correct answer is the passage about the chocolate milk. This did nothing but take away from the buildup of the scene, and it added no importance. Exactly how does chocolate milk relate to the mean streets? If drinking chocolate milk is indeed important to the story, then it should be placed more strategically, not plopped into narrative about the mean streets of Los Angeles. What was the importance there? There was none.

In another story—which was well written and plotted—the author made one critical error: the author added the use of symbolism, which repeated several times in the story, without the meaning being shown at the end. There was no connection at all. The author of that story managed to keep this repetition clean and focused, so each time the symbolism reappeared, it felt fresh. The critical error was in never making the connection between the symbolism and the story. When asked why the connection was never made, the author replied that he couldn't figure that part out. He also stated that several people had questioned him about it prior and more and more he was regretting that decision. He assumed no one would really catch on to it, but they did, and one reader wrote about it online in a negative review.

In my previous novel, there is quite a bit of symbolism. In the editing process, I was asked to expand on the symbolism to ensure that it all made sense in the end. The more I revised, the more I found passages to sneak some hidden meaning into. As asked and advised, all of the symbolism was either explained or made clear to the reader by the end of the story. What I loved about that is, one reader said she reread the book to rediscover all the symbolisms, clues, and inferences that she had overlooked in the first reading. What was more interesting was that she found meaning in so many things that I didn't plan to have meaning in … but she, as the reader, saw it.

The book has many references to the words "box" and "dark." These words can be easily overlooked as they are ordinary words that don't raise repetition flags, which was my plan. By the end of the book the reader should have been able to make the connections with the words and the emotion of the protagonist. The symbolism revolved around two main features: an animalistic-like female and a Chinese coffin. When the protagonist finally faces what he has been suppressing for years, these symbols take on a deeper meaning and are brought to light. Everything eventually ties together and the reader should have been fulfilled, not wondering what it all meant. Had I spoke of the animal like female or the Chinese coffin on different occasions but never tied them in at the end, it would seem these symbols were put in for absolutely no reason other than to fill space and mislead the reader, which is how the original story was written.

Being able to bring all the symbolism to fruition took hours and planning. It is not enough to simply place an item or thought somewhere in your manuscript, these items must be properly placed at the correct times. You must also keep track of the items you have used to infer importance, as they will need to be explained later. If you repeatedly refer back to a broken red vase in a mystery novel, then the purpose of the red vase should be brought to light at some point.

Every symbol should have meaning. Sometimes, there is so much going on in a story that you can easily forget what was placed and where. For situations such as these, you should keep a book log to track what, where, and when an important item was written into your book. Do not overlook items written into the early chapters of your book. Occasionally, you will have a brilliant idea in the later chapters of your book, to ensure a fluid use of symbolism or reference to importance, you may need to go back to earlier chapters and add some clues leading up to those in the end.

Don't be put off by having to go back to earlier chapters to add in importance. Most writers would tell you they have gone back to earlier chapters to add in passages which clarify items or thoughts in later chapters. The important thing to remember is, if you add anything that infers meaning, you must also bring that meaning to light in some form. Do not under estimate your readers and their ability to find connections within your story, or their ability to discover you left some important connections out.

Stick to asking yourself these questions: why is this important to my story, and how does it tie in to my story? When your manuscript is complete ask yourself this: did I tie in all the symbolism and explain all the connections which were inferred? If you kept a running log, then go back and double check your items to make sure each one has an explanation. No items should be left unanswered, except in the case of cliffhangers which will be explained in the next book in a series.

Your task as an author is to read the first chapter of your manuscript and remove at least five sentences that have absolutely no meaning. Remove erroneous details which distract from the heart of the story. Start a log book which details when an important item or thought was placed in your book, when it comes up again, and when it is justified. Remember to ask yourself: why is this important to the book?

The problem: inferring importance that does not pan out.

The solution: make sure every idea, action, or object you present is critical within the story, has a meaning, is explained, or ties in in the end.

The problem: forgetting what ideas were previously planted in the reader's mind.

The solution: keep a book log.

Do's & Don'ts:

Do add symbolism when it will be revealed later.

Don't add symbolism that leads nowhere.

Do use a book log.

Don't forget where you added symbols or ideas.

Do leave a symbol as a cliffhanger when writing a series.

Don't leave a symbol as a cliffhanger if it will not be explained in a later book.

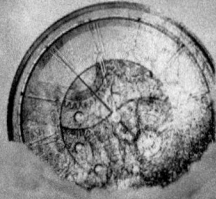

Section 16: Branding
ALL RIGHT, ALL RIGHT...WE GET IT ALREADY

What is branding? For the purpose of this book, and in strict regards to writing, branding is the use of including a brand name within a story.

Branding has become a hot internet topic over the past year, it can be seen all over and is usually done without the intent to do it. For example; a couple standing on the beach, wearing t-shirts with a brand name logo, post their picture to their social media wall. By placing a picture with a name brand showing, the couple has exhibited a form of branding. This is usually harmless and often times unintentional. Another set of friends take a picture by the bon fire holding up cans of name brand alcohol and post it on the internet: branding.

A high school kid posts an update that he just ate ten bags of Doritos: branding by publishing the name brand of the chips. In fact, I just used branding by naming the specific brand of chips. In movies and magazines, these showings of brands tend to be deliberate as they are endorsements. The movie, *Wayne's World* did an excellent job of spinning their endorsements in a spoof scene where they put down branding, yet at the same time named or showed all of their endorsements. Other examples of branding show characters in the movie, *The Italian Job,* driving Mini Coopers. The hosts of *American Idol* display cups with the Coke label on them. Odds are if a name brand is clearly shown on television, film, or a magazine it was placed there for endorsement and monetary purposes. There is typically a contract behind this type of branding as these are paid endorsements.

Branding is quite different in relation to a novel. Authors must be cautious when using brand names in a story. It's possible to be sued for libel should a company feel they have been depicted in a way they deem bad for public relations. In one scene of my book, I clearly stated that Travis grabs a can of Coke and chugged it down to help with his migraine. The Coca-Cola company was not degraded in that statement so branding was not an issue. In fact, they were given free advertisement. If I had said something negative about the company, then it goes without saying that a lawsuit may not be far behind.

Why give a name brand if it's such a hassle? Because it brings familiarity to a story and it also makes a story more believable.

Example with branding:

Travis reached into the fridge and pulled out an ice cold can of Coke. This always worked for his migraines in the past.

Example without branding:

Travis reached into the fridge and pulled out a can of cola. This always worked for his migraines in the past.

Example without branding:

Travis reached into the fridge and pulled out a refreshment ...

Which example was more realistic? How many people call soda, "cola?" Does calling it "cola" feel generic? Does calling it "a refreshment" sound stuffy? Sometimes branding brings a realistic feel into the story and can also add to the date of the book. Other times it begins to sound plain pompous when over used.

Example of overusing branding:

The Jaguar purred along the highway at speeds reaching 135mph. Mason relished the Jaguar's plush leather interior. As he continued down the highway, he saw a Caribbean blue BMW with strict pin striping above the wheel wells. He gripped the steering wheel on the Jaguar tighter and took pursuit of the blue BMW, but the BMW was to quick. In the rearview mirror he saw Kristen following close behind in the titanium gray VW CC. The CC was no match for the Jag, but she gave it a go. Suddenly the BMW, the Jaguar, and the CC were side by side on a two lane road. Mason hit the brakes and the Jaguar came to a screeching halt. Moments later the CC was drifting around the Jag.

Argh! Enough already. No need to "name drop" so much unless there's a car company doing some serious endorsement payments here. If this continued throughout the book it would become infuriating to a reader. This is branding and name dropping to an infinite degree and it takes away from the story. Readers see these vehicles as characters, and unless the story is told from the car's POV, the car only needs to be named once. It doesn't matter if this is a spy story, a love story of an heiress, or a thriller about a prince on the run, this extreme repetitious name dropping becomes boring and distracting, and ultimately begins to feel like an advertisement.

To resolve this problem, use the name of the car one time and then refer to it as the car each time after. This keeps the reader in the action. By stating the brand one time, the reader gets a picture in his head that sticks. Repeated use pulls a reader out to where he only sees a car and not the story. With so much emphasis on the cars, it is only logical that the reader would be distracted from the actual story.

Reread the example of the cars above. Answer these questions? Name two of the cars in the scene? Now name the two characters named in the scene? Did it take you longer to recall the names of the cars or the characters? Were you aware there was a chase occurring? Or, were you so focused on the cars that the chase scene was secondary?

In order to keep a reader enticed, don't distract with shiny things.

On a side note, my editor pointed out that that particular example was over exaggerated and felt way too forced. My rebuttal: that scene was inspired by an indie book I read, except the author of that book wrote about a different mode of transportation, and I did change the entire scene. However, I used the exact same amount of branding as the author did within the same amount of sentences. A few weeks later, I came across a book with similar branding ... this type of name dropping is out there, and it is occurring in indie books.

Example decreasing the amount of branding:

> The Jaguar purred along the highway at speeds reaching 135 mph. Mason relished his speedy machine and the plush leather interior he had imported. As he continued down the highway, he noticed a BMW, the color blue like a Caribbean ocean, with strict pin striping above the wheel wells. He gripped the steady steering wheel tighter and took pursuit of the car, but it was too quick. In the rearview mirror he saw Kristen following close behind in the titanium gray Volkswagen CC she had loved more than life itself. It was tricked out but was no match for his Jag, yet she gave it a go. Suddenly the BMW was side by side with the other cars on a two lane road. Mason slammed the brakes bringing his car to a screeching halt. Moments later Kristen was drifting around him, and kicking up dust.

Some of the brand names may have been repeated but only for the purpose of distinguishing it from a crowd of three. It may be necessary to say the name more than once for the need of discriminating between several vehicles, but the brand name shouldn't be tossed out so haphazardly that the reader feels like he is in a commercial. Imagine there is a quota to how many times a brand name can be used, then try to use it five times less than that. Find synonyms for the word "car," and use those intermittently. Also, be aware that shooting off exotic names that aren't well known may also distract from the book. In one book I read, I had to stop reading to search for images of the vehicles and then I became intrigued and forgot to go back to the book.

Know your audience. There's nothing worse than hearing, "This book is right up your alley," and discovering it's a book on military tactics riddled with names of weaponry some military agents never heard of. This may not be right up Susie Homemaker's alley — who was born and raised in middle-class suburbia. Mrs. Homemaker likely doesn't know these weapons, and will lose interest if they're repeatedly mentioned by brand. She has no clue what they are, so stop forcing them on her. You may be thinking, "So Mrs. Susie Homeworker shouldn't read my book. That'll solve that problem." Don't disregard her so quickly, Mrs. Homemaker may love reading military espionage books, but may not love expansive branding or having to look up a million different types of weaponry to keep up.

Ask yourself this: does branding add to or take away from my scene? Does branding make my story realistic or sound pompous? Did I depict this brand in a negative way?

Using a name brand can also date your material. By using the name Instagram, the reader will know you are writing a story sometime after 2011, since Instagram came in around that time. If you write about taking a Polaroid picture, a young reader might not know what you are referring. The term, "take a Polarioid," hasn't been used casually in over a decade, and the branding may date your book.

When writing about a story set in current times, talking about something such as Plasma television may date your book in the future. Case and point, I found a story I wrote years ago but couldn't remember when I wrote it. While reading this story, I came across a passage that spoke of the character listening to a new cassette tape of Culture Club she purchased. This immediately dated my story back into the eighties. Then it spoke of the skaterboarders who were sporting their pristine Vision Street Wear t-shirts at a party. In my personal case, I can date this book to somewhere between 1986-1989, when I listened to Culture Club and was introduced to skateboarding.

Do you see how using a particular name and brand can date your book? If that story was in print today, many kids now may not have a clue about this band or what name brand Vision Street Wear was. Be careful when branding: what was high fashion yesterday might not be today. Also, a particular brand used today may be obsolete in a few years. Do you think teenagers in 2020 will know what dial-up is? These are things to keep in the back of your head.

The problem: use of too much branding or name dropping.

The solution: use brand names sparingly. Do not be a show off by name dropping more than necessary.

The problem: dating your story by branding.

The solution: try not to use too many fly-by-night brand names if you don't want your book to be easily dated.

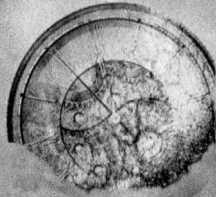

Section 17: Branding, Copyright, Trademarks
CAN THEY SUE ME FOR THAT?

Can you be sued for branding, copyright, or trademark use? The answer to that is not easy or cut and dry. Each subject must be addressed on its own.

Now that the pesky problem of name dropping has been resolved, what are the legal ramifications for using a brand name in a book? It all depends on how you use it. The only name dropping I did in my previous book, was in naming "Coke" as the drink Travis had during a migraine episode. The brand name wasn't depicted in negative context, therefore I feel safe that there will be no lawsuit pending.

The key here is to watch how you portray the context of the brand. Any negativity can result in a libel suit from that company. What is libel? According to most law dictionaries, libel is defined as written defamation. What does this mean for you? If you write a book and use a brand name in such a way that the company considers the use its name as a defamation of the company, they can sue you.

Conversely, any positives are free advertising. Naming a book within your book is a type of branding. Give a bad review to the point the author feels his book sales may be hindered and there is a lawsuit in the making. If it's worth the suit then proceed, but carefully weigh this decision as a libel suit against a person or company can get pricey. On a side note, this can be inclusive to blog posts and social media posts according to one literary attorney. Libel is all-encompassing to anything in writing. Know your rights as an author, but also know your boundaries and the effects of pushing those boundaries.

On the other hand, if you would like to give my book a wonderful review in your book then by all means, carry on. This would be free advertising on my end and not something I will scoff at. The important thing is to give credit where credit is due, otherwise you may be infringing on another author, and that is a whole other lawsuit. What you can't do is quote an entire page of my book without explicit written permission. This begins to infringe on copyright laws.

Back to the topic at hand: it's nearly impossible to write a book without product placement at some point. The world is surrounded by name brands, but you should choose wisely as to how they're used. And don't forget, branding can also date your book.

All of the above holds true for a trademark which is what a brand name's logo is generally covered by. A product brand name is usually not trademarked, but their symbols, such as the Nike "swoosh" logo, or type of lettering or distinctive characteristic may be. These things are trademarked and legally protected from use without permission. It's okay to mention a trademarked company in a book, it's not allowable to place the logo in the book without obtaining the proper permissions first. Placing the logo without permission can get an author into a world of legal woes.

How does this differ from taking a picture with a logo showing and posting it to the internet? This question has been such a hot topic and widely publicized during the SOPA scare. Ultimately, your picture posted to the internet is not for sale. If you show a logo in your book, and your book is for sale, you have infringed on a trademark. Again, this is a gray area that remains in the courts. There are lawyers who specialize in this kind of stuff, and there is so much information to be learned that I couldn't possibly go into it all. Besides that, this is not an area I want to get into lengthy, legal terminology in. To be safe, if you absolutely must depict a logo then acquire the proper permission, otherwise refrain from using a picture depicting a brand name. Also, stay up to date on what the latest issues in branding are for authors.

A copyright is different than a trademark. A copyright protects a written work from infringement. Things such as manuscripts, lyrics, and movies all fall under the copyrighted umbrella. The title of a book or song is not copyrighted, however. Which means you many mention a book title without permission, but it would also be wise to mention the author. This also means the title of your book might also be the title of a book previously written and one yet to be written. You may not use the name of a prominent title to misrepresent your own book as someone else's. For example, you can't put out a title called, *Baking Cakes for Dummies,* using the same type of cover design to mislead readers into thinking your book is part of the *For Dummies* collection of books.

If you wanted to put out a book titled *Baking Cakes for Dummies*, first you must learn if the *For Dummies* title is trademarked as it may be a trademarked conglomeration. Yes, a name can be trademarked from others falsely representing themselves in congruence with that company. In fact, reference to the word *Jedi* must be properly researched, as it is covered by trademark protection in various uses or forms of the word. You may not use the word to misrepresent yourself, website, or product among other uses as being somehow affiliated with Lucas films. Here is my disclaimer: This book is in no way affiliated with Lucas Films, and use of the word was only used to depict an example of trademark protection, not to improperly misrepresent myself as an affiliate or associate of Lucas Films.

Another thing you can't do is directly quote a book for the purpose of fiction, but you may allude to certain scenes or passages. If you have permission to reference a passage, then that must be noted in your book. Quoting directly from another person's work without permission or giving proper credit is called plagiarism. Stick to only referencing a book or work if in doubt of how much of it you can actually use.

Example of referring to a book:

> Kelly laughed at the kids. "Remember that scene in *Lord of the Flies* when they first landed?" she asked.

This is permissible. What an author doesn't want to do is give away the entire plot, the same as you would not want someone else to have a spoiler in their book. Direct quotes of someone else's book may not be written for the

purpose of general fiction or non-fiction without permission. Lyrics from songs may not be quoted. There has
been much speculation about whether a few words can
be written, and according to the United States Copyright
Office there is no clear cut, black and white answer to this
question. Their best advice is to obtain permission when
intending to quote lyrics of a song or a lengthy passage
of a book.

The purpose of this section was not to add more questions, but to advise you that there are certain legalities
you must be aware. When it comes to being sued, being
oblivious to the laws may not be enough to save you. As
a writer, you assume certain rights and responsibilities for
the content of your book. Write responsibly.

The problem: inappropriately using copyrighted
or trademarked material.

The solution: when in doubt, get permission from
the owner of the brand, item, or material. Do not
make false accusations or misrepresent an item,
and do not make derogatory remarks about an item
unless you have the money to back-up the lawsuit.

For more information on trademarks:
www.uspto.gov
For more information on copyrights:
www.copyright.gov
**For an interesting read on a
trademark infringement lawsuit:**
http://news.cnet.com and search Lucas Films lawsuit.

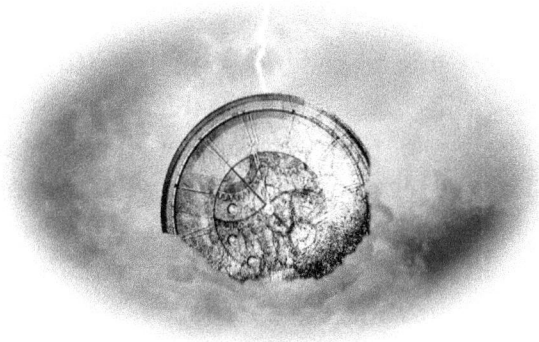

Section 18: Dialogue Tags
SHE SAID. SHE YELLED. SHE ASKED.

What is a dialogue tag? A dialogue tag is a word or set of words that are used following dialogue set in quotes.

Example of dialogue tag:

"This is not the time or place," Trisha said.

The "Trisha said" part is a dialogue tag. This tag is quite important to the statement which is why this is also at the top of the list for rookie author mistakes. This is a quickly growing list, don't you think?

The most common mistake is to add too much narrative after the active dialogue. As a new author who committed this mistake repeatedly, I can honestly say that I did it to enhance the emotions of the character. It didn't feel like enough to simply say "she said". As an author, I felt like my creative genius was being held under water. It made no sense why such a mundane rule would be put up to impede the flow of a story. My characters needed more emotion, more substance, and sometimes that came after active dialogue. Then I was educated.

Most the books I have read over the years are books published by the larger publishing houses or their subsidiaries; as such these books have been edited for content and grammar. It never occurred to me that traditionally published authors didn't use erroneous narrative after active dialogue. Is this a true fact? Yes. Go back and read a section of any traditionally published book with active dialogue and read what it says before and after the dialogue. Odds are it only uses the words, "said," or "asked."

The next logical question is to ask "why?" This is a matter an editor had to continually pound into my head, and though I didn't agree, I conformed to publishing standards. Yes, I gave in to "the man." I figured he was more knowledgeable than I was in this matter, but I still held my reservations. Then it happened, the little white light popped on while reading an independent author's book. Everything the editor said to me was true: too much dialogue after a quote removes a reader from the flow of the dialogue. This may lead the reader to forget what the dialogue was about when it picks back up again after numerous other details have been told.

Example:

"This is not the time or place," Trisha said with a lofty glare weighing down her furrowed brows. "You had no right to show up to my place of business," she shouted, her face red as the sun. "If you don't remove yourself right this second, I'll have security called and have you arrested for trespassing," her voice was loud but managed to crack, sounding coarse as she shoved a finger into his puffed chest.

This grows tiresome when dialogue is written like this for two-hundred plus pages. The active speaking is stopped to explain what Trisha was doing, looked like, and sounded like. Adding these breaks between dialogue stops the flow of the dialogue. Trisha is obviously upset, so the dialogue should flow through her anger without breaks so the reader stays in the emotion of Trisha. With the lengthy, wordy breaks in between, the reader is removed from the build-up of the scene to read detail. This may seem minor to a new author, but this can get a manuscript sent back or rejected in a query.

The fix is very simple: use one action word after the active dialogue (dialogue tag) or add active narrative prior to the dialogue. Don't break up active dialogue unless something or someone has made a drastic change that necessitates a break.

Example with proper dialogue tag:

"This is not the time or place," Trisha said. "You had no right to show up to my place of business. If you don't remove yourself right this second, I'll have security called and have you arrested for trespassing!"

Notice only the word "said" was used, but an exclamation mark was added at the end to denote her anger. This keeps the dialogue flowing smoothly and keeps the reader focused within the correct realm of emotion throughout the read. All the filler (fluff) is gone and only the important dialogue remains.

Example with active narrative prior to the dialogue:

> Trisha furrowed her brows and gave a lofty glare. Her face was as red as the sun and voice so loud it cracked. With a finger shoved into his puffed chest, she began her verbal assault. "This is not the time or place. You had no right to show up to my place of business. If you don't remove yourself right this second, I'll have security called and have you arrested for trespassing!"

In this example, the author wanted the reader to get a visual picture of what Trisha looked and sounded like before the dialogue began. This may be important if Trisha is normally a passive person. Using the descriptors before the dialogue allows the reader to take a mental picture and move on into the dialogue after. There is debate as to whether this is fluff or creativity. The best way to handle this is to decide whether the detail adds to the scene or fills space. Some passive narrative may be okay, but be sure not to go overboard. It's probably safe to thin out some of the passive narrative above.

Remember: show, don't tell.

Example with a break in between:

> "This is not the time or place," Trisha said. "You had no right to show up to my place of business. If you don't remove yourself right this second, I'll have security called." She shoved a finger into his chest, "and have you arrested for trespassing!"

This scene doesn't flow well with the break, but it's used to show where a simple break can be used and for what purpose. Sometimes a break can be used to show a pause in dialogue, a time where the characters aren't saying anything or contemplating their next words. In such a case, passive narrative such as, "Trisha stopped to consider the words to follow," would state this. Try to avoid going into the character's thoughts in a break too much, save that for the next paragraph. Keep dialogue with dialogue, and use passive thoughts as a new idea after the active dialogue has come to an end.

A dialogue tag is different than dialogue action. Dialogue action states, "she hissed," "she stammered," "he grumbled. These should not be used after active dialogue, or used as sparingly as possible. The reason is, when too much dialogue action is used it begins to take away from the dialogue preceding it. Most readers tend to read over dialogue tags because they are so common. By doing this, a reader remembers the active dialogue and overlooks the dialogue tags. But, when dialogue action is used, it takes away from the substance.

Example of dialogue action:

"Don't yell at me," Lynn screamed.
"I'll do what I want," Kevin hissed.
"Give me a break," she groaned.
"Why don't you take a long walk off a short bridge," he muttered.
"Screw you," Lynn hollered.

With all those dialogue actions, the reader can become more engrossed in the actions after the dialogue than the

actual dialogue. Do you see how over use of dialogue actions can take away? Readers see action that needs to be
processed, which over shadows the important dialogue.
See how the correct use works much better.

Example of correct dialogue tags:

> "Don't yell at me," Lynn said.
> "I'll do what I want," Kevin replied.
> "Give me a break!"
> "Why don't you take a long walk off a
> short bridge?"
> "Screw you," she yelled.

Can you see how changing the dialogue tags allow
you to read more of the active dialogue? The dialogue is
the meat and potatoes of the sentence, it should not be
spoiled with fillers. Keep in mind what part of the sentence harbors the most importance. That is the part that
should receive the greatest attention from the reader.

Your assignment: take an active dialogue scene from
your own book and do a rewrite. Try using a traditional
dialogue tag such as, "she said." Then try using active
narrative before the dialogue. Finally, try putting in a
break using passive narrative. Remember, more narrative isn't always better. If the two previous paragraphs
explained how in love the characters are, then it's not necessary to fluff the story with more active narrative about
how in love they are between active dialogue. It's already
implied. Keep it simple and to the point.

The problem: using too much narrative after or between active dialogues.

The solution: stick to basic dialogue tags: he said, she answered, he asked, etc. Do not use passive narrative to give so much detail between active dialogues that the reader forgets what the dialogue was about in the first place.

Section 19: Back Story
HOW BACK IS TOO FAR BACK

What is back story? Back story consists of all the events that led up to why the characters are who they are, which may include family, upbringing, hometown, work, past loves, past hurts and things of that nature. It's anything that leads up to where the story is today.

Think back to questions you would ask in an interview: who, what, where, when and how. These are the questions you must ask when creating a back story. This is where a character gets his or her personal characteristics from or would lead him to be the way he is today. This is one area of writing where things have changed over time. Go back and read novels that were written in the early 1900's, mid 1900's, and late 1900's. One thing which has vastly changed over the decades and into the twenty-first century is in the area of the back story.

In the early 1900's, the back story was written out in great detail at the beginning of the book. This allowed the reader to know the time period, the scenery, what has led up to the start of the book, and often times of the back story of the major characters. This could go on for several chapters which was the norm during this time. Over the decades, but most notably in the later part of the 20th century, back stories began to drop off and become replaced with an abrupt induction into the book.

The industry now states that the twenty-first century reader no longer wants to be plagued with details about things that have nothing to do with the story, or back story that is so long and cumbersome they may become bored before ever getting to the meat of the story. Nowadays, most editors will advise a writer to refrain from starting a story in the past with a mundane back story. The trend is to start in the action. Simply drop the reader smack into what is happening now, and move on at full speed from there.

Is there still a need for back story? Absolutely, except now the author should incorporate this back story throughout the novel. Show, don't tell. Allow the characters to voice what's significant about the past, or make it an active narrative. Don't simply devote a bunch of pages to tell the reader what happened in the past, allow the reader to experience the past through the characters. Let them talk about what has happened, or what is so important about the back story that led the character to be the way he or she is today.

For instance, an early 20th century novel may describe a farm land, the government, and a family lineage before going into the story of a young woman born into wealth who vowed to change women's equality. To this story, all the political background and her family's disposition would all be relevant to the person she is, or who her family thinks she should be in this case. A reader might assume a young woman born into wealth would have no cause to fight for women's equality, but the rest of the story would hit on why she is fighting.

Place this same story written in 2012, the story would not have two chapters of back story. Instead it would start with the young woman arguing with her father because she wants to make a living on her own, not live off a trust fund. The story would progress, and at several points, she would talk or think about watching her mother waste away as a servant to her husband and tending to her womanly duties within the home. The main character would think about not being able to realize her own secret dream of becoming a lawyer due to the politics of that day and age.

For this particular story, the back story will be incorporated into the running storyline and the novel should move forward. At times, more information about her past will be strategically placed in the story, until the reader has full comprehension of who the character is and why.

This isn't a strict rule as many stories have flash backs which give back story. However flashbacks are treated differently than back story, because these flash backs should be shown and not told to the reader. A back story is usually told over time, not shown.

Take for instance the first time a man meets a woman. They go out and talk on the first date giving their back story: who they are, where they came from, what brought them to California, what led up to becoming an engineer, or whatever their stories are. This back story gives a lot of information and insight into how they got to where they are today.

Example of back story:

My name is Tania L. Ramos, born and raised in the inner city of Los Angeles, in a small gang infested community called El Sereno. I was raised by a single mother who did her best to provide, but that meant she was usually gone at work. My role in society was a latchkey kid who literally had a key wrapped around her neck.

I moved on to junior high but opted to take the city bus over forty-five minutes into a different school district. I spent the next six years on that same route going to middle and high school, succeeding in every creative writing, writing, and journalism based class, yet failing every standardized English course. In junior high, I was elected class treasurer and was given a scholarship to attend the USC University Young Author's Program. In high school, I took acting, creative writing, journalism, leadership, computer-aided drafting, and eventually lettered in swimming.

Every day after school I would go home to take care of my little brother. I hated it. Let me reiterate: I *hated* it. I had no life outside of school and felt like a parent at a very early age. After high school I took some college courses, but my life was forever redirected after getting pregnant at the age of 20. So many plans were put on hold, including plans to become a paramedic and start writing.

Readers now have some insight as to who I am and why I am this person, although there are years of history left out. This is my back story and what I would tell someone on a first date. It lets them know a bit about me and, if I added more back story, would bring the guy up to speed to who I am today. Back story can be long and drawn out or short and sweet. Adding back story throughout a novel is different. It's more of a second or third date, and sometimes even like years into marriage when a couple discovers something new about each other. It's when your spouse says, "I never knew that about you. That explains so much."

This happens almost every day in life. It's when someone who knows me forever discovers I have a terrible fear of butterflies and asks why. I have no clue why, except a recurring dream of butterflies attacking me, their little tentacles dripping with blood. Still gives me the chills to this day, but do you see how that's showing? That was me actively telling you about my inner fear. The previous information about me was more like reading a bio, which is telling—and is often times very dry, like a drawn out back story.

One big complaint about new authors is related to the telling of back story. This is where a twenty-first century author can catch up to the times. Start with action, or at least some forward movement, and integrate the back story so readers will say, "Oh, that explains so much." Don't give away everything in the beginning. Leave some mystery to be unraveled throughout the book to keep the reader engaged and constantly learning about the characters.

The problem: giving too much back story early on.

The solution: develop the back story through the character and throughout the book.

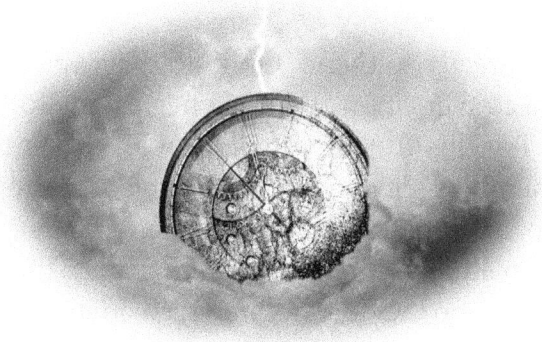

Section 20: What's In a Name?
OVERUSE OF CHARACTER
NAMES IN DIALOGUE

Giving a name to a character is very important, this is the first impression we get from the character and it speaks worlds of information before anything else. Think very careful when deciding on a name. Don't make it too complex or something a reader may have a difficult time pronouncing. There's nothing worse than never really knowing what the character's name is. Consider this name, Madeleine. Not too difficult. Now consider this name, Madeelyne. Maybe you were able to pronounce them the same, maybe not. How about Jorja? Did you read that as Georgia?

Also, consider picking names that don't sound alike as this becomes confusing: Maggie, Mary, Mendy, and Margie will become confusing after a while if they are all characters within the same book. Instead, choose very different names: Maggie, Eleanor, Kathy, and Paulette. This will help avoid confusion.

The next problem is over using a character's name in dialogue. For the next day or so run this little experiment: count how many times you use a person's name when speaking directly to them. Only do this experiment during casual conversation and not when asking for a specific person. Try this during a lunch break, when talking to family members, or during any other casual encounter. Outside of an initial greeting, how many times do you say that person's name directly to them during the course of the conversation? Odds are, not very often. Yet, authors take this liberty in writing.

Many new authors haven't been versed in the art of creating believable dialogue. This is a learned trait, but with time, can be caught before it's ever written. During the course of a normal interaction—minus initial greetings—a person rarely says the other person's name in dialogue. It's clear the person being spoken to is the person on the listening end, therefore their name does not need to be repeatedly mentioned. Usually, when their name is mentioned it's in a scolding or negative manner, such as a mother scolding her child using all three given names.

When creating believable dialogue, an author must write the way conversation is actually spoken. Do a bit of people watching and copy down conversations. Review this dialogue later in the day and see how messy it is. Incomplete sentences, grammatical errors, and so on are all part of typical dialogue. What's missing is the repeated use of names.

Example of using names too often:

"I know Jeremy, but I had to come find you," she said.

"Ely, if you would have just called—"

"You know I couldn't call. Jeremy, I had to see you face to face. I had to know," she said.

"This could have all been avoided, Ely. This big scene. I tried to save you," he replied.

"Jeremy, if you would just let me explain—"

"I can't do this anymore. You mean the world to my family, Ely, just not to me. Goodbye."

The above example is a sample of common dialogue, with the extensive use of first names. This is not an exaggeration, but something I have come across first hand in more than a dozen indie books. This is not believable dialogue and should be avoided at all costs. So why is it so widely used? Because, it adds a dramatic element. As stated previously, the use of first names is often used during heightened times of emotion in real life. We use this to make a point and add severity. This automatically instills the sense of something dire. In literature, an author wants everything to be important. What this actually does is distract from the real dialogue with filler and a false sense of urgency, not to mention it comes off as fake. If every active speaking part had a name plugged into it, it would slow down the flow. Read the above example again and then read the corrected example below.

Example, removing the extensive use of names:

"I know Jeremy, but I had to come find you," she said.

"If you would have just called—"

"You know I couldn't call. I had to see you face to face. I had to know," she said.

"This could have all been avoided. This big scene. I tried to save you," he replied.

"If you would just let me explain—"

"I can't do this anymore. You mean the world
to my family, just not to me. Goodbye."

Without all of those names being thrown around, the
dialogue has a smoother flow. The words carry on without names being randomly interjected, disrupting the dialogue. The reader is aware of the speakers and doesn't
need a constant reminder. Allow the conversation to
progress the way a normal conversation would progress,
glance back at those notes you took when people watching and see how the character's dialogue compares with
real dialogue. How many times does the use of a first
name come up in real conversation compared to that in
your book's dialogue?

The problem: over using names in active dialogue.

The solution: if it's clear what characters are
speaking, then avoid using their names unless it is
to make a strong statement.

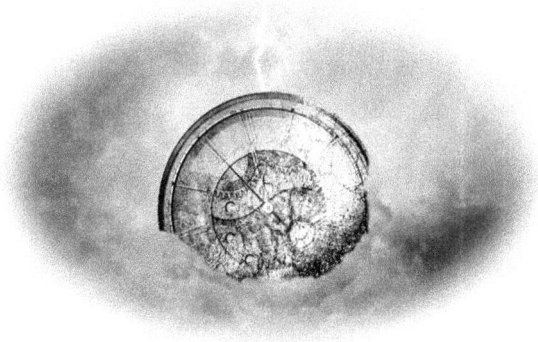

Section 21: Being Assertive
NO MORE INDECISIVE CHARACTERS

What is meant by having an indecisive character? This occurs when an author does not make the character assertive. In effect, the character comes off as indecisive or wishy-washy when he or she shouldn't.

This is an all too common and often an over looked error in writing. Many editors miss this or don't bother to comment on it at all. With the narrative of a story, it should be a violation to have an indecisive character. The story is from a character's POV after all, and who knows better than the character? Allow the character to have an assertive opinion and stand up for it. When an author is wishy-washy, then the character will be as well. Being indecisive also lends to the author's own insecurities. Count me guilty as charged in this area. As an author it's my goal to appeal to the masses. I don't want to step on any toes or offend readers with the opinions of my characters—which are not always my own. Yet sometimes it's necessary to step out of my body and into the character's, as all writers must do. When in conflict about how readers will react to the thoughts of a character I tend to give options in effort to diffuse a situation or lash back.

Example of an indecisive character:

> There was nothing about the Democrats that Phil liked. He hated having to sit there and pretend to care, but that was his job until he worked his way up. Ten minutes into the speech he decided they were all full of themselves or just confused. He prayed, or something like that, it would all end soon.

It's not in my nature to want to offend readers, especially if this isn't a shock factor book. So, instead of outright declaring what Phil thought about the Democrats, I instead chose to water it down with the line, "... or just confused." That line totally diffused what Phil really thought, which was "they were all full of themselves." This shows a weakness in the character as well as the author.

Then, in an effort to not offend every non-praying religion or atheists, I played down the next sentence by stating, ". . . or something like that," instead of declaring the fact that Phil is a praying kind of man. Those extra words are not only unnecessary fillers, but they are confusing. The author must take a stand for his character because nobody else will. The character is only as decisive as the author allows him or her to be. The reader may sit there and wonder, "Doesn't the character know if he was praying or not?" Once again, don't give the readers cause to leave the scene as this pulls them out of the story.

An author may defend that Phil's character is not too wishy-washy. Okay, but that still begs the question: doesn't he know if he's praying or not? Be wary that if he has been portrayed as a vocal man who holds no punches back, then this is very out of character. It's not reasonable for an author to hide behind a character. Characters should have flaws, but these imperfections should not be rubbing off from author insecurity (unless it's an autobiography). There are very bold books out there with very harsh opinions coming from the character. There's dialogue which may make some readers blush or become upset. This is the point though, for writing an engaging novel, to instill certain emotions in the reader.

My next book in the works deals with a man who's a real jerk and makes pretty derogatory statements to a woman he impregnated. At first, I made him bad but from a safe distance. The more I read and reread, it became obvious that I was holding back because I didn't want to upset a reader, and this was killing the story. Ultimately, I had to make this guy as bad, unruly, and vocal as possible. My goal was to create a character that readers would love to hate. Creating this character could not be done to the fullest extent if the character was down played due to my need to not upset certain readers. However, if this character were given full range of my imagination then some men and women will take offense, and that's the point.

Don't mistake a fictional character's voice as the author's opinion. Not every character can be perfect and please every reader. There should be conflict and different points of view among characters. Don't be afraid to stir up a little drama. It's what makes it feel real. I must state to my boyfriend almost every time I read him a passage, "the characters in this story are not based on actual events and are not real people. The opinions of the characters don't necessarily represent the opinion of the author, the two should be seen as completely separate entities where the character is nothing more than the creativity and imagination of the author, not an alter ego."

Example of a character with solid ideas:

There was nothing about the Democrats that Phil liked. Absolutely nothing. He hated having to sit there and pretend to care about their pompous agendas, but that was his job until he worked his way up. Ten minutes into the speech he decided they were all full of themselves and couldn't tell their head from their rear end. He prayed to God that it would all end soon, that God would smite the entire Democratic Party with a brimstone hail storm.

See how the character comes off as much stronger? Try to avoid using the word "or" which portrays a weak character, unless the character should be shown this way. One common complaint throughout the internet regarding new authors is that they (new authors) do not take a firm stand with their characters. The speculation is that a new author is afraid to offend potential readers and future followers. Don't fall into this category, take a stand as an author, and give the personality that the character is intended to portray.

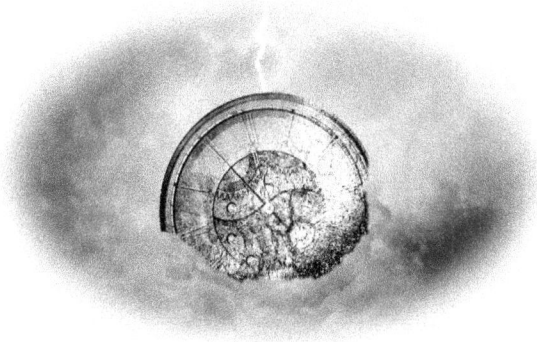

Section 22: Characterization
BUILDING THE PERFECT PERSON

What is characterization? Characterization is how the author describes a character in her book, including personality traits and background information. This is valuable information to the book to make a character appear real. Readers are searching to relate to real characters and see themselves through them, and in this day and age, a reader wants to feel connected.

Think back to a few decades ago when only perfect women and men were portrayed on the big screen. It made for great movies but left watchers feeling inadequate compared to the characters in the movie. Producers caught on to this and more recently started showing everyday men and women on the screen. Sure they still use beautiful people, but more and more average people are appearing at the top of the credits. And why? Because, viewers want to relate.

In this same thinking readers want to relate. It's not advisable to have a perfect woman or man, one without flaws, one with the perfect body, the perfect hair, and face. Characters like this can become an immediate turnoff to a reader. How often in life are there truly flawless people? How many people can you count that are without any imperfection? Take a moment and dwell on that question; count the neighbors, spouses, in-laws, friends, the people you work with, then take inventory on how many lack a single defect.

Everyone knows at least one beautiful woman or handsome man, but are they without fault in all aspects of life? Are they beautiful on the inside as well as the outside? Most people have a fault somewhere. It is imperative that every character have their faults in order to come off as believable. This makes a character much more relatable and engages a reader further into the story.

Imperfections don't necessarily have to be physical characteristics, but should be strong in deeper personality traits. Drinker, smoker, compulsive liar, at odds with one's self, talks too much, too shy, too pushy, push-over, there are so many traits to choose from. These faults should be realistic and play into the flow of the story. It's not enough to simply say, "Jade is incapable of commitment." The author should show that Jade is incapable of commitment. In fact, even if it's never directly stated that Jade has this issue, the reader should be able to make this distinction through the showing rather than telling.

What's critical is keeping track of the characters. Two books I have come across change characterization midway through the book. Things such as, the female had hazel eyes then she suddenly had blue eyes, or a character changed careers, is noticeable to a reader. It's understandable how this happens. Perhaps it took the author years to write the manuscript and forgot the character traits, or perhaps the character changed in the author's mind and forgot to go back and make crucial changes.

Whatever the case, it's critical to keep track of characters. There are many character worksheets available on the internet. These guides are an easy reference for authors. They provide categories such as physical traits, back story, job, family line/siblings, and so on. Many of these sheets are free and should be utilized for a quick and easy guide. Authors aren't perfect and make many mistakes, but don't allow an abrupt change in characterization to be one of those major errors.

Beyond backstory, two types of characterization exist: Direct and indirect. Direct characterization is shown when adjectives are used to directly describe the character. This is the easiest form of characterization and people do it all the time in real life. For example, if asked to physically describe your mom words like, "tall, slender, short, pudgy, round face, narrow eyes, red hair, brunette," might be said. These are direct characterization points. This type of characterization is important to character development as it gives the reader an idea of the person the author is trying to create.

What is not needed is a quick rundown of every physical trait in one sentence. Leave a little to the imagination allowing the reader to create the character throughout the first few chapters. Let the reader not only learn the physical traits but also the indirect traits (qualities) which add to the overall appearance of the character.

Indirect characterization is when things such as values, qualities, and physical traits are shown rather than told. Using indirect characterization brings more depth to a story and allows the reader to use more imagination. With direct characterization an author tells about traits, but in indirect the author shows rather than tells about the

character. Examples of both direct and indirect characterization are shown below.

Direct characterization:

Betty was not only tall and slender, but she
had deep dimples on each cheek matched by one
on her rounded chin.

Indirect characterization:

Betty dropped a check for thirty dollars in the
charity bucket and smiled gracefully at the young
boy ringing the bell. Once she donated half a
paycheck to a fellow co-worker whose home was
lost in a fire.

Is the difference clear? One gives a direct portrait of
the character while the other lends to the kind of character
Betty is. There is no set time frame to write about these
traits, however, it's advisable to let a reader know what
the character looks like within the first few chapters. The
reader should not picture a tall, thin, brunette throughout the entire book only to be told at the end that she was
short, thin, and blonde. This is a complete disservice to
the reader and will leave them jaded.

Indirect characterization can also be intermingled
with physical characteristics, although not considered direct characterization. This is a way to imply something
about the physical characteristics of the character in the
book. Doing this is as simple as making an implication, or
indirect remark, which gives the reader information about
the character. The converse becomes true about giving

direct characterization about the character's qualities and values. It's all in the telling or showing.

Direct characterization about qualities:

Betty was a generous woman. She was not only generous but a humanitarian.

Indirect characterization about physical traits:

Jim glanced across the room to see Betty's petite blue jeans lying out on the floor. They were so small had he not known better he would have assumed they were for a child.

In the direct characterization example, the reader is told that Betty is generous and a humanitarian. Nothing is left to the imagination as this is a stated fact. Refer back to section fourteen to review showing and telling. This is an example of telling. Note, not all direct characterization refers to physical traits alone.

The second example explains indirect characterization through showing the reader about the size of pants Betty wears. The reader creates an image in her mind about what size the character is, although never directly told that Betty has a size two waist. Again, this refers back to showing rather than telling.

Characterization is one of the fundamentals an author must truly master. It's not good enough to have a fantastic story, but it needs to be told appropriately and hold the reader captive. Without believable characters the reader can relate to, a potentially fantastic story is essentially lost to lack of creativity. There is a wealth of information on the internet regarding how to build characterization. This is one of those topics that an entire book can be built around. This manual is in place to make you aware of key topics of interest and hit on them. Characterization is very important, please do more research if this is an area you are unfamiliar with.

The problem: keeping track of a character.

The solution: keep a journal/log of all characters

The problem: telling too much detail all at once.

The solution: don't always tell the character traits or personality, sometimes you must show them. Tell about the physical characteristics early on.

For templates on characterization:
www.educationoasis.com/curriculum/GO/character_story.htm

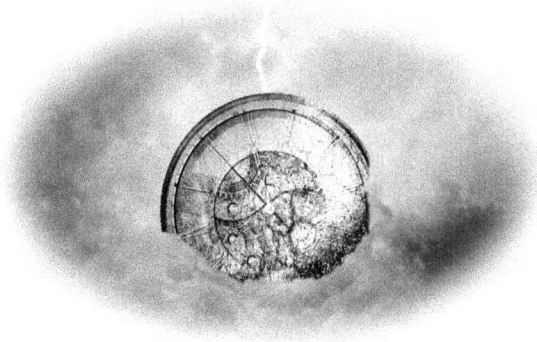

Section 23: Period Based Stories
A DIFFERENT ERA

What is a period based book? A period based book is actually a book set in a specific time which is not the current era

A popular genre is period, or time based, with themes such as medieval, turn of the century, or stories based in Renaissance times. With so much history behind us, it's no wonder many authors are turning to writing period themed books. Why is this so important that it require its own section? Because so many authors get it wrong.

Some books talk about medieval times with references to Roman armies or the eighties with reference to plasma televisions. These things did not exist within these time frames, and many readers will pick up on this. If you are going to take on the task of writing about a time and place you do not know about, then you must also assume the burden of doing the research.

Time pieces offer a bit of history. Though the location may be fiction, the time frame is not. The only exception to the rule is in telling a story about an unknown future. That's the only time an author may take liberties with cre-

ating an era. Outside of that, all material should be true
to the time frame. Everything down to dialect and slang
should be used with caution. It's not wise to have a Roman guard say, "Hold up and show I.D." This isn't something he would say.

Think on this: what is the target audience for a piece
set in medieval times? Probably the exact same audience
who has read previous medieval works and who watch
medieval time based movies. This audience probably
knows a thing or two about the period and will spot a
fraud quickly. These are also the same readers who leave
reviews. An angry reader will leave an angry review and
point out all of the flaws in the book. Some online re-
viewers will pull apart a book piece-by-piece and word-
by-word. If a period piece isn't convincing be prepared
for the worst.

Simple things such as push button phones were
not readily available in the 1970's, so don't say a hippie
punched in the number to call a friend. Do not mention
a Gatling gun for an 1830 piece. Something as simple as
placing a Dodge Charger back one year before its time will
blare out to any car junkie. And with all that, the author
loses credibility and audience.

In order to maintain a feel of the time frame, an author must be immersed in that time. Research, research,
and research some more. Read other books based in that
era. Watch documentaries of that time. Find any and all
information possible pertaining to that era, and confirm
its valid information from a reliable source. If necessary,
have someone who's an authority on that era do a proof
read of the manuscript solely for misplaced items or dialect of that given time.

Example of improper time frame for Christ:

> The Roman guard stopped the man and said, "Hold up. Tell me your name."
> The man stopped and offered a hand saying, "I am Matthew. I'd like to attend the stoning, he stole my sister's virginity."

Unless that story is a parody or spoof, the dialogue isn't believable.

Example of correct time frame for Christ:

> The Roman guard held up his hand and said, "Hold. What is thy name?"
> The man stopped and removed his tattered hood saying, "My name is Matthew from Israel, son of Canaas and cousin of the tax collector. I have come to see the man called Ares stoned as he has brought shame to my sister."

This is a more believable dialect and use of period based language.

Getting language and wordage correct isn't easy for the first time author taking on this challenge. Again, it becomes imperative that the author do relentless research before publishing the manuscript. Any item, right down to a horse and buggy, better be placed in the right time. The best bet is to research all items written in a period based book. Find when they were invented and when they were obsolete. Yes, even obsolete items can ruin a book. For example, a Polaroid photo is a term rarely heard these days. A rag sheet isn't something typically heard in the 1990's. And though these terms may come up in dialogue or reference, they shouldn't come up as things readily used.

Example of an obsolete term:

Marty sat at the coffee table reading the rag sheet his wife left out. It was June 12, 1998 and after losing his job, the only thing Marty looked forward to every morning was the paper.

Example of the corrected obsolete term:

It was June 12, 1998, and after losing his job, Marty only looked forward to reading the paper every morning. He sat at the coffee table and smiled at remembering his grandfather calling the newspaper the rag sheet right up until the day he died.

Example of twenty-first century obsolete term:

Casey saw the car crash and instantly took a Polaroid.

Example of twenty-first century obsolete term, corrected:

Casey saw the car crash and instantly fumbled for a camera. All she could find was an old Polaroid that her mother used to use.

Any misplacement of terms or items will be as apparent as that black sheep after the snow storm. Readers tend to stay in one genre due to that fact that they know the material well. Don't assume the wool can be pulled over their eyes, to have them take you seriously, you must take your work serious. Don't forget to do in-depth research on the topic, era, and items at hand. This will separate the serious authors from those who didn't take the time to do the research. You will want to stand apart from those who didn't do the work.

The problem: misusing objects or language in a period based manuscript.

The solution: do the research and make it count. Get a second opinion from someone knowledgeable on the period.

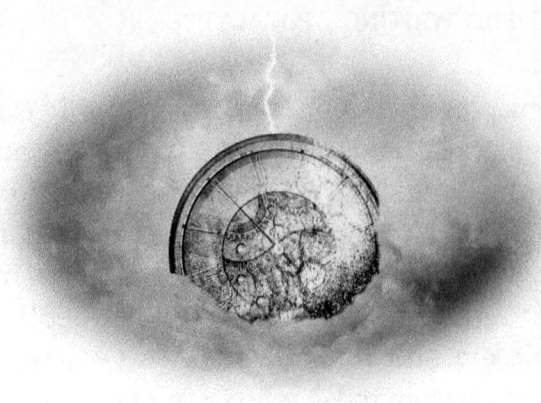

Section 24: Editors
WHY WE ALL NEED ONE

Authors, please pay special attention to this section!

I implore you, for the courtesy and reputation of self-published authors everywhere; please have your manuscript edited before having it published. The old adage of one bad apple ruining the entire barrel is very much true in the world of publishing.

For the past few years it never occurred to me why self-published authors had such a bad reputation. There was a lot of debate floating around the internet. Publishing houses alluded that authors had to pay their dues, while authors believed publishing houses were being snobs. Maybe it was a bit of both, but those are speculations.

Self-publishing has increased over the years and continues to look like it's on the rise. Even major distributors such as Amazon.com have seen the call for self-publishing and created their own venue for authors to do this. This year, Penguin took over Author Solutions and bought out one of the biggest online assisted publishing companies, not to mention the large amounts of small no-name or independent companies popping up simply to market a few books. The problem with all these companies is that although they suggest having a manuscript edited, none of them *require* it to be edited. An author pays to have a book published, the publishing company takes that money and creates a book whether it's edited or not. Other companies allow authors to upload a book for free, and again no editing is required. Some have standards as to what they won't publish, material and content wise, but that's more of a matter of taste in the book than in editing.

Why harp on the editing process, especially for indies? Simple: one poorly written book can reflect on every other indie book. Two bad books nearly seal the deal on the perception of *all* indie authors if read by the same person. First impressions are everything, even with readers who may take a chance on an indie book.

Imagine the book you have written is amazing and meticulously edited, but a reader states, "All self-pub books are horrible. I've read two and their editing was atrocious. Sorry, I'd like to read your book, but I just don't read self-pubs anymore."

Those words have been whispered around me at indie events. I've heard them in bookstores and at some more prominent book events. It's saddening to be judged by the lack of concern from others in the field.

Editing isn't cheap. Most full length manuscripts can start at a fee of $3,000 and go up from there, depending on the number of words or pages. Manuscripts are the reflection of an author, and it doesn't matter if you majored in English or have an MFA degree hanging over the computer: all manuscripts need to be edited. There are errors you, as the author, will miss because you will read over missing words or overlook misspelled words. The reason is, you know what it's supposed to say, and may look passed an error rather than pick it out. Often times, it's merely simple errors that are missed, but those simple errors are picked up by readers, agents, and publishers.

This book is intended to assist authors of every genre on how to fix content errors, but not grammatical errors. It shows what should be done and doesn't imply an author will get it right the first time. One cannot depend solely on self-help books to create a flawless manuscript. Authors need editors. Self-published authors need editors to keep up the standards of books with those of traditionally published books. We can't complain that indie books are overlooked or given a bad name if these books are indeed published because an author was able to take a pen to paper but not seek invaluable editing services.

There are several alternatives to paying high end prices to editors: have several friends read and edit, have an English major read it for a smaller fee, use other authors, even try beta readers. In any case, this should be done by more than one person. The more readers you have, the better. The better the manuscript, the better received by the public and by publishing houses if an author is doing queries to traditional publishers.

The problem: overestimating your own self-editing abilities. Not using an editor.

The solution: if you have the funds, hire a professional editor. If you lack the funds needed, try using beta readers (next section).

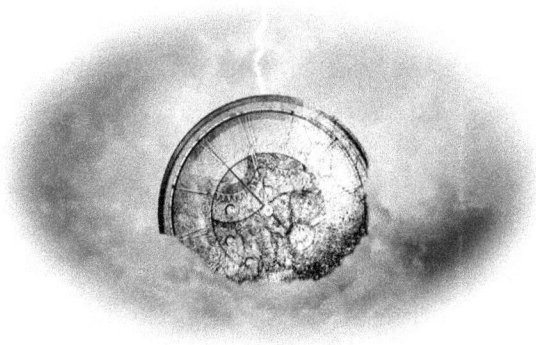

Section 25: Beta Readers
TWO PAIRS ARE BETTER THAN ONE

What is a beta reader? A beta reader is one who reads a work (usually fiction) with the strict intention of giving strong critical opinions of the manuscript.

Beta readers may be a term that has crossed the ears of many authors, but there are those who have no clue who these precious reading gems are. They give advice to grammar, story-line, and/or characterization. Often times they highlight these areas on the manuscript and then give a summary of things to be improved. Some are so computer savvy that they will mark areas on a Word document within the margins for the author to make changes.

Several sites on the internet provide links to beta readers within specific genres. *www.fanfiction.net/betareaders/* is one such site with some of the highest numbers of beta readers, each separated into sections such as anime/manga, books, movies, games and so on. This is not a commercial for this site and I bear no affiliation with them, but it's one I have personally used, so feel confident enough in speaking on.

What an author (also known as the alpha reader) does is pick a beta reader or two or three. It's advised to pick at least two since nobody is perfect and two minds are always better than one. This also lends to the fact that two readers will always have different opinions, and see things differently and, as I have learned, sometimes pick out things the author never knew existed within the story.

What to expect: brutally honest opinions of the manuscript. If a beta reader thinks it's awful they'll let you know, but a good beta reader will also give you ways to improve. Often times the opinion isn't solely based on whether or not they liked the book, but whether they feel the flow was appropriate to the reader. They do try and generally give unbiased opinions, except to those that immediately pertain to grammar, characterization, and flow. However, be prepared to hear that the characters weren't believable, the story line is foggy, or questions were left unanswered. Be prepared to hear the same honesty that a paid editor would give.

Your next question may be: how much do beta readers cost? Sometimes, nothing! Many don't charge, and those that do have asked for far less than traditional editors. For beta readers who do charge, it's imperative that the author ask for references. Some beta readers are students studying the field and merely ask for you as a reference or that they may later refer to being a beta reader of a manuscript. It's advisable to keep track of which beta readers were used for which particular manuscript. As stated, many don't charge. So why do they do this? Many simply love to read while others like being on the front lines of new and emerging stories and authors.

How to pick beta readers? First, if you are in a writer's club that has beta reader (critique) groups, try that option

SURVIVING THE WRITING APOCALYPSE

first. The reason being, many groups can get together face-to-face with you and ask questions or go over concerns. Having this time allows you to answer questions or make clarifications and also allows you to ask the beta reader questions for suggestions or improvement. One-on-one, or within a group, can offer valuable assistance over simply receiving a written report that can sometimes be misconstrued or read with the wrong tone.

If the only option is to use an online beta reader, then research the best sites to be used. There are many credible sites out there, and many have references or author statements listed. Choose carefully, if the manuscript is a specific piece set in 18th century England, then the beta reader should be one who reads fiction with a subcategory in 18th century period themes. If the book, such as my book *Be Still*, which is fiction based on the relationship of a father and son, was to be read, then I would first search under fiction, then English language followed by the subcategories of general fiction, family, and emotional.

Each site uses a different technique for searching. Be sure to ask the beta readers how many manuscripts they have read. Of course it's difficult to determine actual qualifications or check on references as many readers are anonymous, but an author can only hope the reader is legitimate. And if the reader is free, then no harm no foul.

When can you use a beta reader? You can use a beta reader at any point during production of your manuscript. Some are willing to read the first few chapters and give advice about context, flow, and direction. Some authors strictly use beta readers when a manuscript is complete, while others use them before sending in a query and others before sending in a final manuscript for publication. Beta readers can be used at any time during the writing process. In fact, many authors now thank their beta readers on the acknowledgments page of their book. This isn't necessary, but some authors feel so strongly about the help and support of beta readers that they give the acknowledgment where it is due.

In this day and age of publishing houses being sterner on signing new authors, and with self-publishing on the rise, it's imperative that indie authors be aware of all of the resources available to create a credible manuscript. This is concurrent with the need to get a manuscript edited. The words, "I can't afford an editor," should never be uttered again when beta readers are readily available by the thousands. There is no longer an excuse.

The problem: not knowing what a beta reader is. Not knowing how or when to utilize a beta reader.

The solution: research! There are many sites out there with beta readers. Remember, a beta reader can be used at any point of the creative process.

For more information try these sites:
www.fanfiction.net/betareaders
www.querytracker.net/forum

Also, try asking people who read your blog, website, or in your writing group to proof your manuscript.

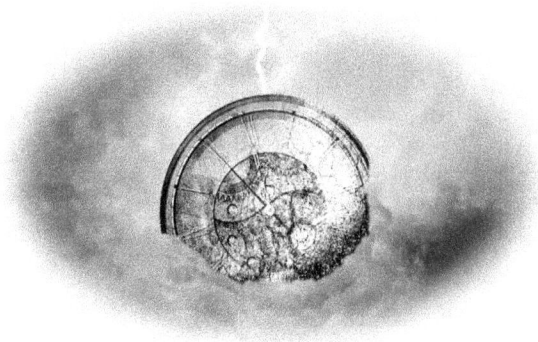

Section 26: Cover Art
EVERYONE JUDGES A BOOK BY ITS COVER

How important is cover art? It's the first thing readers see, that makes it almost as valuable as the story within.

Cover art is the very first marketing item readers will see. If your cover is all black with white letters, then your title better be pretty catchy. Most cover art designers would say the cover should represent your story without giving it all away. Let the cover be the first symbol of your book, one a reader will uncover later in the book.

Do not simply upload a picture from a royalty free website and run with it. This is okay to take bits and pieces or to alter the photograph, but know this: you may not be the only person to use this photo. I have come across a few book covers that utilize the same picture. Although this is perfectly acceptable since the art was purchased without obtaining exclusive rights, it didn't make the authors feel confident in the originality of the book cover.

Another issue to keep in mind is that your book is most definitely judged by its cover. Think about how many books you were drawn to based on the cover alone. Have you ever been drawn to the title of a book but turned off by the cover art? Visit your local book store, or just browse an online bookstore, does the art work play into whether or not you would spend money on that book?

The mentality works like this: if you took the time to have cover art properly done, then you probably took the time to write a well-written book. Shoddy cover art may lead a reader to think the subject matter inside isn't any better. That does come off as harsh, but it's the truth. We judge by the cover of products all the time. This is why big businesses pay big money to have their art work done. I'm not saying you have to drop thousands or even hundreds of dollars on your art work, but if this is something you can't do you on your own, please seek outside expertise.

As an indie author, I would ask that you look into an independent company to do your artwork if needed. Again, this is something which requires research on your part, but will be worth it when you have a first class cover. Do not be so hasty to publish that you forget this important item. Readers will not get to your story if they can't get passed the cover.

The problem: a poorly presented cover

The solution: get professional help where needed, and do not be in so much of a hurry to publish that you skimp on the very first thing a reader will see.

Need cover art? Think of all the small businesses out there which offer competitive rates and quality work. If you are an independent or self-published author, please look into giving your business to other companies which, like you, are taking a chance in a competitive world.

Want more information:

The power of colors:
http://www.buzzle.com/editorials/1-13-2005-64166.asp

Looking for cover art:
http://www.blueharvestcreative.com,
createspace.com, bookcoverpro.com*

Other sources include:
the publisher you will use,
graphic & design schools, online tools

*Surviving the Writing Apocalypse is not, and does not, endorse any of these companies or its affiliates. These companies are listed for reference purposes only and were found either using a search engine or by recommendation from other independent authors. Please research any company you choose to use.

Section 27: In Closing
BRINGING IT ALL TOGETHER

So much of writing includes research, no matter what the genre. In researching for this book one thing was abundantly clear: there aren't many books like this out there. I found a multitude of grammar books, a few books on characterization, some on plot, and a plethora on marketing, advertising, and how to sell online. The question was posed by my editor and myself, "Why aren't there more comprehensive books about self-editing for content and mechanics on the market?"

While that question plagued us, and though we searched and searched but only found a few books out there (many outdated), I continued to write and research for this. The answer to that question only hit me after reviewing the manuscript for the second time, one thing was quite clear throughout each chapter: although there are stringent guidelines to learn, there are also authors out there who don't follow the norm and become quite successful. Recall that most sections in this manual end with, "this is sometimes the authors voice," or, "these are merely guidelines."

Writing is a creative process, and as such only you can truly know your voice. Only you will know whether these guidelines can or should be crossed. And only you know your comfort zone. With that being said, do not let guidelines impede your work or hold back your genius. Many well-known authors are known for breaking the barriers and pushing the lines. But, keep this in the back of your mind, does your book break barriers and challenge the system?

Your manuscript is an extension of you. Let your creativity flow, yet be knowledgeable in what mainstream publishing is looking at if that is your route for the future. Perhaps you are an indie or self-published author, then I implore you to raise the bar. Learn all the lessons given within this manual, it's not enough to master one part of this book; a well-rounded author must be able to put every piece of this book together to build the greater picture. To survive in the twenty-first century of intricate writing, you must be armed with the appropriate tools to rise above the masses of self-published authors. It's not enough to simply possess these tools, but also to be able to put them in use.

By utilizing these tools and mastering them, you will set a standard and raise the bar. These skills set you up for being taken seriously by readers, fellow authors, and possibly by publishing houses. With the correct resources, even a bad story written well would still be seen as well written, as opposed to a poorly written bad story. Keep in mind that not every novel is destined to be great. Not every author will be a bestseller. Not every author will rise to fame. And, not every book will be a runaway hit. However, by putting all of the pieces together, you can have a well "written" book.

My advice: now that you have read the guidelines of content and mechanics, go write your book. Don't worry too much about getting it right in the first round. We all make mistakes. The important thing is to finish your book. If you can remember some of these lessons during the writing process that is excellent. If not, catch the problems in the first round editing, and second, and third. Writing is a process. Editing is part of that process. Learning from your mistakes makes the process easier next time.

Good luck and remember: you can do this. Go get those readers.

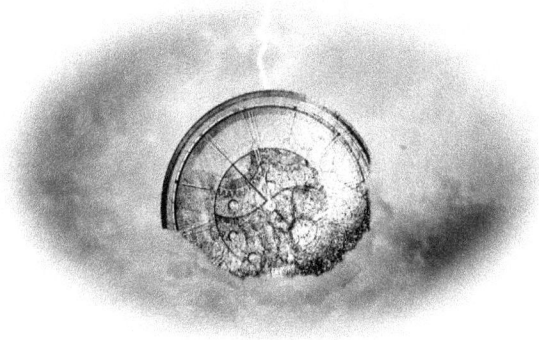

Section 28: Checklist

Now is the time to put everything you have been taught into action. Utilize this list to ensure you understand each section and have mastered these skills.

Point of View

- What is my POV?

Head-hopping

- My scene stays in one POV?

Author Intrusion

- I've avoided an omniscient feel

Foresight

- I've removed all things that look into the future that the character can't possibly know

Scene Breaks

- I've created scene breaks for changes in POV

- Scene Breaks in Time

- I've made scene breaks when the time or place has suddenly changed to tell a different part of the story

Bold

- All bold lettering has been removed from my manuscript

Capitalization

- The use of all capital letters does not exist, except to directly show how a note or sign is written

Italics

- Italics are used to show change in dialogue

- Italics are used in appropriate referencing

Repetition

- There aren't repeating scenes in my manuscript

- All repetitive words have been changed

Show & Tell

- There's an equal balance of showing and telling

Inferring Importance

- Everything written is relevant, important, and explained

Branding

- There's not excessive use of product placement

Copyright & Trademarks

- No product has been defamed in this story

- The use of ©, ®, and ™ are not used after product placement

Tags

- Dialogue is marked with simple tags, "said, replied, asked . . ."

Backstory

- My backstory isn't given all at once but spread throughout the course of the manuscript

Names in Dialogue

- I have refrained from over using the character's names in active dialogue

- My characters names are easy to pronounce

Assertiveness

- There isn't indecisiveness among the characters unless that is the character's trait

Characterization

- There's an equal amount of indirect and direct characterization

- The character develops throughout the story, not all at once

- The character has relatable flaws

Period Pieces

- All elements referenced in the story were available during that time

- The dialogue/words are true to that time

- There's no mixing of time periods

- I have researched this time and location

Beta-Readers

- I will look into having at least two beta readers before publishing

My Vow:

I realize having an editor is as important as writing this manuscript. This story deserves to not only be read, but my readers deserve to have a well written book. My name, and therefore my reputation, is attached to this book which holds me accountable not only as an author, but as an author who represents the proud group of indie authors. As such, I will demand perfection in everything I produce and encourage other authors to do the same.

Do you have what it takes to survive the writing apocalypse?

So you think you have what it takes to survive the writing apocalypse? Show us your work at The Writing Apocalypse website (www.WritingApocalypse.com) and your book may be featured as a top listed book on our site. See the website for more information on how to have your book considered as a writing apocalypse *survivor*. Books are judged by our panel based on the guidelines listed in this book as well as editing for grammar. We do keep an open mind for those one-of-a-a-kind books that break all the rules and make it work. We also have features such as downloadable forms for book logs, characterization, outlines and more. The website offers more features for authors with more questions, or needing a one-to-one consultation.

Thank you for taking the time to read this manual and raising the bar.

The Staff at Writing Apocalypse

About the Author

Tania L Ramos is a practicing registered nurse as well as an author and entrepreneur. She works full time at a hospital in her community in Southern California's High Desert. On her downtime she raises three children, runs a household, and somewhere in there finds time to write novels. Writing has been her first passion for as far back as she could recall and intends to continue to follow her calling. "When I Thought I Was Tough," is her first experience in novel writing and can be read free on Bookemon.com. Two time award winning, "Be Still," is her second novel which takes a look into the life of a man caught between living and dying, with fun, dark fantasy scenes into the mind of a man in a coma, and also follows the life of those he has left behind. This story has been quoted as being, "a real ter jerker," and "answers the questions we have been too afraid to ask out loud." Tania has three projects on the table: a scifi teenage alien novel, another family filled tear jerker, as well an editing book.

Tania also finds time to help other authors with creating trailers for books. She blogs on a personal

WordPress site as well as with her local High Desert Bloggers. And every second Saturday of the month she can be found at the High Desert Chapter of the California Writer's Club (hdcwc.org). To date she has been engaged in several meet and greet events as well as a blog tour and several signing events. See her events page for all future events and for a contact form to invite her to your special venue.

www.ingramcontent.com/pod-product-compliance
Lightning Source LLC
Chambersburg PA
CBHW060243050426
42448CB00009B/1571